WHEN DID EVE SIN?

The Fall &
Biblical Historiography

JEFFREY J. NIEHAUS

LEXHAM PRESS

When Did Eve Sin? The Fall and Biblical Historiography

Copyright 2020 by Jeffrey J. Niehaus

Lexham Press, 1313 Commercial St., Bellingham, WA 98225
LexhamPress.com

Print ISBN 9781683593997
Digital ISBN 9781683594000
Library of Congress Control Number 2020935612

Lexham Editorial: Elliot Ritzema, Abigail Stocker, Danielle Thevenaz
Cover Design: Lydia Dahl
Typesetting: ProjectLuz.com

For

Kristen Ashley Montgomery

ἐκλεκτῇ κυρίᾳ

CONTENTS

CONTENTS

ACKNOWLEDGMENTS

Sir Isaac Newton wrote in a letter: "If I have seen further it is by standing on the shoulders of Giants."[1] However "far" the work that follows may have seen or penetrated into a question of biblical interpretation or into the historiographical issues that question may imply, it does so only because I have been the beneficiary of many interpreters who have gone before. The one who started me on this road was Meredith G. Kline, but along the road there have been many others. I will not name them here because the list includes every biblical interpreter named in the pages that follow.

I make this acknowledgment now because in the course of this study it will be clear that I have disagreed with almost every interpreter considered in this monograph who has addressed the questions raised by Genesis 3:3 vis-à-vis Genesis 2:17. It has not been easy to do so and also is not a task that I relish or would want to undertake again. For the sake of a thorough consideration of the data, however, I have felt I owed it to anyone who would read this monograph not simply to assert one point of view but to review what others have said and to consider in detail any problems their arguments may have raised. I hope any reader will find that where I have disagreed I have done so in an open-minded and even-handed way even while, as I hope and believe, I have been guided by certain interpretive principles that are generally recognized.

---

1. Isaac Newton, letter to Robert Hooke, 1675, https://digitallibrary.hsp.org/index.php/Detail/objects/9792#.

CONTENTS

CONTENTS

ACKNOWLEDGMENTS

S ir Isaac Newton wrote in a letter: "If I have seen further it is by standing on the shoulders of Giants."[1] However "far" the work that follows may have seen or penetrated into a question of biblical interpretation or into the historiographical issues that question may imply, it does so only because I have been the beneficiary of many interpreters who have gone before. The one who started me on this road was Meredith G. Kline, but along the road there have been many others. I will not name them here because the list includes every biblical interpreter named in the pages that follow.

I make this acknowledgment now because in the course of this study it will be clear that I have disagreed with almost every interpreter considered in this monograph who has addressed the questions raised by Genesis 3:3 vis-à-vis Genesis 2:17. It has not been easy to do so and also is not a task that I relish or would want to undertake again. For the sake of a thorough consideration of the data, however, I have felt I owed it to anyone who would read this monograph not simply to assert one point of view but to review what others have said and to consider in detail any problems their arguments may have raised. I hope any reader will find that where I have disagreed I have done so in an open-minded and even-handed way even while, as I hope and believe, I have been guided by certain interpretive principles that are generally recognized.

---

1. Isaac Newton, letter to Robert Hooke, 1675, https://digitallibrary.hsp.org/index. php/Detail/objects/9792#.

ACKNOWLEDGMENTS

ABBREVIATIONS

BDB	Francis Brown, Samuel Rolles Driver, and Charles A. Briggs. *A Hebrew and English Lexicon of the Old Testament*. Oxford: Clarendon, 1904.
BT 1	Jeffrey J. Niehaus. *Biblical Theology, Volume 1: The Common Grace Covenants*. Bellingham, WA: Lexham Press, 2014.
BT 2	Jeffrey J. Niehaus. *Biblical Theology, Volume 2: The Special Grace Covenants (Old Testament)*. Bellingham, WA: Lexham Press, 2018.
BT 3	Jeffrey J. Niehaus. *Biblical Theology, Volume 3: The Special Grace Covenants (New Testament)*. Bellingham, WA: Lexham Press, 2019.
CTJ	*Calvin Theological Journal*
DCH	David J. A. Clines and John Elwolde, eds. *The Dictionary of Classical Hebrew,* vols. 1–8. Sheffield: Sheffield Academic Press, 1993–2011.
HALOT	Ludwig Koehler, Walter Baumgartner, and Johann J. Stamm. *Hebrew and Aramaic Lexicon of the Old Testament*. Trans. M. E. J. Richardson. Leiden: Brill, 1994–1999.
JBL	*Journal of Biblical Literature*
JETS	*Journal of the Evangelical Theological Society*
VT	*Vetus Testamentum*
WTJ	*Westminster Theological Journal*
ZAW	*Zeitschrift für die alttestamentliche Wissenschaft*
ZNW	*Zeitschrift für die neutestamentliche Wissenschaft*

Introduction

A QUESTION OF
HISTORIOGRAPHY

This book explores a historiographical issue, but it is not a treatise on historiography. It does not explore historiographical questions that may arise or have arisen regarding history in general or the Bible as history. Even if such a thing were possible, a study of all conceivable or existent historiographical phenomena would not be necessary to reach the goal the present work hopes to reach.

Before stating that goal, it is important for me to note one assumption that informs this work, since no work is without assumptions. The present work assumes the historical accuracy of those things the Bible presents in a straightforward way as records of actual events and what the people involved in those events did or said. With respect to biblical history (and moreover to all biblical genres) I affirm the inerrancy of Scripture.[1]

The goal of this monograph is to understand how Genesis 2:17 and 3:2–3 stand in relation to one another. A comparison of the

---

1. Biblical inerrancy is understood to mean the original autographs of the Bible were without error. For a classic presentation of the doctrine, see "The Chicago Statement on Biblical Inerrancy" online.

verses raises one issue in biblical historiography: the phenomenon of laconic reporting of an event by a third-person omniscient
narrator (the historiographer) followed by a first-person retelling
of the same event (also recorded by the historiographer) that adds
further information not provided in the first account.

THE PURPOSE AND GOAL

A longstanding question about Genesis 3:2–3 vis-à-vis Genesis 2:17
motivates the present work. Most writers in the history of biblical
interpretation have thought the woman added (in Gen 3:3b) to what
the Lord had said (in Gen 2:17b) when she told the serpent that she
and her husband were forbidden not only from *eating* the fruit of the
tree that stood in the middle of the garden but also from *touching* it.
The present work proposes a different view: the woman did not add
to what the Lord said, but rather she gave further information not
supplied by the historian in the earlier, laconic account in Genesis 2.

THE METHOD

This study logically entails three avenues of approach:

1. Genesis 2:17 and 3:2–3 should be compared in their
   own right.

2. The woman's response to the serpent should be considered in light of any New Testament comments on
   her behavior.

3. We should compare the proposed understanding of
   the relationship between the two passages with other
   cases of what may be similar historiographical phenomena in the Old and New Testaments.

These three avenues of approach inform the present work. Along
with the exemplars, the history of scholarship regarding each case

will be germane to our discussion. Although it would be almost impossible to locate and interact with every scholarly comment ever made on the issues encountered in the pages that follow, it has been my goal to take into account representatives of the views generally held—and repeatedly and even traditionally held— regarding Genesis 3:3 vis-à-vis Genesis 2:17 during their long history of interpretation.

THE CASE STUDIES

The proposed exemplars are: (1) the Genesis 2 and 3 accounts already mentioned, (2) the Genesis 12 and 20 accounts of Abram and Sarai and Abraham and Sarah (respectively), (3) the Lord's statement to Isaac in Genesis 26:5 vis-à-vis the Abrahamic material spanning Genesis 12 through Genesis 22, and (4) the three accounts of Paul's Damascus road experience in Acts. The study will consider whether each exemplar or set of reports demonstrates the same historiographical phenomenon: laconic reporting of an event by a third-person omniscient narrator (the historian), followed by a first-person retelling of the same event (also recorded by the historian) that adds further information not provided in the first account.[2]

HISTORIOGRAPHIC OBJECTION

Once one sees what exemplars are proposed, one might easily make an objection: historiography in New Testament days was different from historiography in Old Testament days. Moses and his contemporaries did not write history in the same way Luke and his contemporaries wrote history. This objection actually entails two parts: (1) the way biblical writers wrote history, and (2) the way their contemporaries wrote history.

---

2. Or, in the case of Saul/Paul, *two* first-person retellings.

To take the second part first: the ancients in different cultures wrote history differently. Anyone who has read ancient history knows that, e.g., Thucydides (c. 460–c. 395 BC) or Polybius (c. 200–c. 118 BC) did not write history in the style or with the goals of, say, the annals of Thutmose III (1481–1425 BC) of Egypt or the annals of Tiglath-pileser I (r. 1114–1076 BC) of Assyria. The assumptions and expectations were different. However, it is also true that the ancients did not write history in the same way the biblical writers wrote history. The Assyrians, Hittites, and Babylonians unabashedly wrote history as propaganda, and they included, mutatis mutandis, accounts of supernatural intervention on behalf of the emperors. Their historical writing took the form of historical prologues in treaties and of royal annals.[3] There was nothing close to what later people would call "objective" history in those documents. Greek and Roman historians, on the other hand, wrote something closer to what we would call "history," and, especially after the work of Thucydides, history concerned itself more with politics and war reported and evaluated on the human plane and less with supernatural elements.[4]

---

3. Cf. discussion in *BT* 1, 3–6; cf. Jeffrey J. Niehaus, "The Warrior and His God: The Covenant Foundation of History and Historiography," in *Faith, Tradition, and History: Old Testament Historiography in Its Near Eastern Context*, ed. A. R. Millard and James K. Hoffmeier (Winona Lake, IN: Eisenbrauns, 1994), 299–312.

4. As Christopher A. Baron, "Greek Historiography" in *Oxford Bibliographies* (online: http://www.oxfordbibliographies.com/view/document/obo-9780195389661/obo-9780195389661-0078.xml) notes: "First, the very term 'history' derives from the Greek word *historiē* ('inquiry') which Herodotus uses to describe his work, and the subject of historical inquiry decided upon by Herodotus and his successor Thucydides—description and explanation of political and military events in the past—remained standard for many centuries." Gunkel no doubt had the Greek historians in mind when he classed the sources of Genesis as primitive and asserted: "Uncivilized races do not write history. They are incapable of reproducing their experiences objectively, and have no interest in leaving to their posterity an authentic account of the events of their times. Only at a certain stage of civilization has objectivity so grown and the interest in transmitting national experiences to posterity so increased that the writing of history becomes possible. Such history has for its

One thing that ancient Near Eastern historiography and biblical historiography do have in common, however, is the covenantal foundation that informs both.[5] The history recorded by ancient suzerains had to do with conquering and making new vassals or reconquering rebellious vassals and restoring them to the empire. Because God made covenants with people in the Bible, it turns out that the same covenantal idea—with God, and not merely a mortal king, as the suzerain—forms the foundation of all biblical historiography.[6] All biblical historiography has to do with God's covenantal relations with people. That is what establishes a commonality between Old Testament historiography and New Testament historiography and thus begins to address the first part of the objection noted above, that "historiography in New Testament days was different from historiography in Old Testament days"—or, more specifically, that historiography in the Old Testament was different from historiography in the New.

UNIQUENESS OF BIBLICAL HISTORIOGRAPHY

Addressing the most important aspects of historiography in either the Old or New Testament includes two aspects: the covenant-centered nature of biblical history and historiography, and the reality of divine providence and intervention in shaping the historical events and the records of those events. I have written elsewhere about the covenant-centered or covenantal nature of biblical history and historiography and argued that the Bible may be aptly

---

subjects great public events, the deeds of popular leaders and kings, and especially wars." Cf. Hermann Gunkel, *The Legends of Genesis*, trans. W. H. Carruth (Chicago: Open Court, 1901), 1–2.

5. Cf. Niehaus, "The Warrior and His God," 299–312.

6. See *BT* 1, 3–6.

characterized as the "annals of the Great King."[7] Extrabiblical historiography in the ancient world barely comes close to such a concept
and only insofar as it always assumes a divine background to human
events. Mostly, the Egyptians, Assyrians, Hittites, and Babylonians
wrote history that was centered on the king.

Although pagan historiographers assumed a divine background
to—as well as divine involvement in—human events, the degree of
divine providence and intervention that shaped biblical history, and
the detailed interaction between the Lord and his people reported
in that history, constitute the most glaring difference between biblical and ancient Near Eastern historiography. The Bible records
God's active and, most importantly, miraculous intervention to a
degree that is unparalleled in the ancient world. The fact that Moses
predicts what signs and wonders the Lord will do before he does
them is unique in ancient Near Eastern historiography. The contest
between Elijah and the prophets of Baal on Mount Carmel is non-
pareil. No pagan prophet ever said such words as Elijah did: "Lord,
the God of Abraham, Isaac and Israel, let it be known today that you
are God in Israel and that I am your servant and have done all these
things at your command. Answer me, Lord, answer me, so these
people will know that you, Lord, are God, and that you are turning
their hearts back again" (1 Kgs 18:36b–37). No pagan prophet is on
record for doing what Elijah did—calling fire down from heaven.
The Hittites and Assyrians rarely recorded divine intervention on
behalf of the king, and when they did, they did not tell us that
anyone foretold what the god was going to do: rather, they reported
some weather phenomenon that was militarily helpful to the king,
and then, subsequently, interpreted that phenomenon as a divine
intervention on the king's behalf.

---

7. See *BT* 1, 3–6; *BT* 2, 278; *BT* 3, 343, 345.

GOD'S INTERVENTION AND GENRES

God's intervention produced historical events, and the reportage of those events constitutes some very unique historiography. Two genres may be cited as illustrations: what has been called the theophanic *Gattung*, and the gospel genre.[8]

THE THEOPHANIC GATTUNG

In *God at Sinai*, I explored what has been called the theophanic *Gattung*.[9] That *Gattung*, or genre, reports the Lord's appearance to a human being with good and revelatory purposes. Because no other god exists and consequently no other god ever appeared theophanically to a human, the biblical *Gattung* is unparalleled in the ancient Near East.[10] The *Gattung* is as follows:

---

8. The phenomenon of theophany and the attendant *Gattung* had been explored, before the publication of my own work on the topic, by J. Jeremias, *Theophanie: die Geschichte einer alttestamentlichen Gattung* (Neukirchen-Vluyn: Neukirchener Verlag, 1965), and by J. K. Kuntz, *The Self-Revelation of God* (Philadelphia: Westminster, 1967). My observations on the gospel genre had been adumbrated but not as fully developed by Meredith G. Kline, *The Structure of Biblical Authority* (Grand Rapids: Eerdmans, 1973).

9. Jeffrey J. Niehaus, *God at Sinai* (Grand Rapids: Zondervan, 1995).

10. For a rare account of such an appearance in a seer's vision on behalf of Ashurbanipal, see Niehaus, *God at Sinai*, 34–35, 37–38. I have argued that the first storm theophany in Genesis 3 is the background even for pagan theophanic concepts and representations: the memory of divine presence and power coming in storm theophany was handed down from the beginning, and theophanic advent was subsequently (though rarely in historical writings) attributed to some pagan deity or other. Cf. Jeffrey J. Niehaus, "In the Wind of the Storm: Another Look at Genesis III 8," *VT* 44.2 (1994): 263–67; the article argues, on the basis of Akkadian and biblical evidence, that what has traditionally been translated "in the cool of the day" or the like (Heb. לרוח היום in Gen 3:8) would better be translated "in the wind of the storm." The resultant understanding would be that, after the fall, the Lord came in a storm theophany to find Adam, his wife, and the serpent and bring them into judgment. See the subsequent adoption of this translation in John Walton, *The IVP Bible Background Commentary: Genesis–Deuteronomy* (Downers Grove, IL: InterVarsity Press, 1997), 32, and in David J. A. Clines and John Elwolde, eds., *Yodh-Lamedh*, vol. 4 of *The Dictionary of Classical Hebrew* (Sheffield: Sheffield Academic Press, 1998), 185.

1. Introductory description in the third person

2. Deity's utterance of the name of the (mortal) addressee

3. Response of the addressee

4. Deity's self-asseveration

5. Angel's quelling of human fear

6. Assertion of his gracious presence

7. The *hieros logos* addressed to the particular situation

8. Inquiry or protest by the addressee

9. Continuation of the *hieros logos*, with perhaps some repetition of elements 4, 5, 6, 7, and/or 8

10. Concluding description in third person[11]

The *Gattung* reports an actual event in the Bible and is thus a historical genre; the same *Gattung* appears, for instance, in the report of a conversation (royal audience) between David and Ish-Bosheth, son of Jonathan, in 2 Samuel 9:6–11.[12]

Because God or sometimes one of his angelic messengers does show up and address chosen humans, and because he does so with beneficial purposes, and because human nature in its sinfulness naturally reacts with fear at such an event, the *Gattung* that documents these advents can portray them accurately whether they occur in the Old Testament or the New. Two examples will serve: the Lord's appearance to Isaac at Beersheba, and Gabriel's appearance to Mary.

---

11. Niehaus, *God at Sinai*, 31–32.
12. Niehaus, *God at Sinai*, 39–41.

THE LORD'S APPEARANCE TO ISAAC AT BEERSHEBA

J. K. Kuntz has outlined the account of Yahweh's nocturnal appearance to Isaac (Gen 26:23–25) as follows:

	Gattung Element	Genesis 26:23–25
1	Introductory description	23 From there he went up to Beersheba. 24 That night the Lord appeared to him and said,
2	Divine self-asseveration	"I am the God of your father Abraham.
3	Quelling of human fear	Do not be afraid,
4	Assertion of gracious divine presence	for I am with you;
5	*Hieros logos*	I will bless you and will increase the number of your descendants for the sake of my servant Abraham."
6	Concluding description	25 Isaac built an altar there and called on the name of the Lord.[13]

---

13. Cf. Kuntz, *The Self-Revelation of God*, 59; also cited in Niehaus, *God at Sinai*, 32.

GABRIEL'S APPEARANCE TO MARY

I have outlined the account of Gabriel's appearance to Mary (Luke 1:26–38) as follows:

	Gattung Element	Luke 1:26–38
1	Introductory description in the third person	1:26–27
2	Deity's utterance of the name of the (mortal) addressee	1:30
3	Response of the addressee	1:34
4	Assertion of gracious divine presence	——
5	Angel's quelling of human fear	1:30
6	Assertion of his gracious presence	1:28
7	The *hieros logos* addressed to the particular situation	1:31–33
8	Inquiry or protest by the addressee	1:34
9	Continuation of the *hieros logos* with perhaps some repetition of elements 4, 5, 6, 7, and/or 8	1:35–38bα
10	Concluding description in third person	1:38β[14]

The *Gattung* is an established genre, and it reports both human encounters, as in the case of David and Ish-Bosheth, and divine-human encounters, as in the two cases shown above. It reports historical appearances of the Lord or one of his angels to humans with beneficial intent.

The cardinal concern in the present study is this: the historical reports take the same form in both Old and New Testaments

---

14. Cf. Niehaus, *God at Sinai*, 355–56.

because the Lord did the same thing in both Testaments. He or his angel appeared theophanically, and such appearances always occurred in similar ways and produced similar results. There is no difference when it comes to the historiography or the historiographical genre involved in either the Old or the New Testament because the Lord was doing much the same thing (in terms of divine advent) *wherever* he or his angel appeared in the historical record. One need not consult the way ancient Near Eastern suzerains caused their historical records to be written or the way Herodotus or Thucydides wrote history in order to understand this essentially biblical genre in either Testament.[15]

THE GOSPEL GENRE

The same is true of the gospel genre, as Meredith Kline recognized some decades ago. The Gospels include biography, and that is certainly a major aspect of their composition; it is also true that biographical material can be found in the Greco-Roman world. But the Gospels are more than biographies. They are biographies of a *covenant mediator*. As such they include redemptive signs and wonders for a covenant people and the formal creation or "cutting" of a divine-human covenant. These elements do not characterize biographies in the pagan world of Matthew, Mark, Luke, and John, for the very good reason that such divine-human "covenant cutting" never took place in the Greco-Roman world. For that reason extrabiblical biographies by the Gospel writers' contemporaries have limited explanatory power vis-à-vis the gospel genre.

The true precursor of the gospel genre, as Kline recognized, is arguably the book of Exodus. Exodus presents the same

15. It is just to call it an essentially biblical genre because it stems arguably from the first theophanic advent of God in history, in Genesis 3, as noted above and argued at greater length elsewhere.

combination of biography and redemptive signs and wonders for
a covenant people and the formal creation or "cutting" of a divine-
human covenant that one finds in the Gospels. It would be better
to say that the Gospels include the combination of those same elements that we find in Exodus, since Jesus is after all the mediator
of the new covenant which has both fulfilled and replaced the old
or Mosaic covenant. He is the new and greater Moses. The point is
that both Exodus and the Gospels are the same *as regards their genre*,
because in both cases the Lord was intervening in our world and
delivering a people by a covenant mediator prophet and bringing
them into the covenant that prophet mediated. As in the case of the
theophanic *Gattung*, the literary content of the historical material in
both Testaments is analogous because God was doing similar kinds
of things in both cases. A comparison of the content of Exodus and
Matthew can illustrate the idea:

Event	Exodus	Matthew
Birth	1:1–9; 2:1–2	1:1–25
Persecution (all males)	1:8–22	2:16–18
Transport from persecution	2:3–10	2:13–14
Flight from royal peril	2:11–25	2:13–14
Return to God's people	4:18–28	2:19–23
Identity of prophet	3:1–4:17	3:13–17 ("my son") 4:1–11 (temptations) 4:12–16 (Isa 9:1–2)
Call of followers	4:29–30a	4:18–22
Initial signs and wonders	4:30b–31	4:23–25 7:8–12:30
Torah on mountain	20:1–23:19	5:1–7:29

Event	Exodus	Matthew
Torah + signs and wonders	25:1–39:42	8:1–25:46
Transfiguration on/from mountain	34:29–35	17:1–9
Covenant institution	24:8	26:28 (blood of covenant) 27:32–50 (crucifixion)
Covenant ratification meal	24:9–11	26:17–30
Consecration of temple	40:34–35	[Acts 2:1–4]
Ongoing presence	40:36–38	28:20[16]

As we consider Jesus the covenant mediator, we see the Son in his lowly aspect. Nonetheless his birth was celebrated in ways the birth of Moses was not, as we read in Luke's account. The Word who became flesh and dwelt among us was celebrated by shepherds at his first advent. God's decision to announce the birth of his Son to shepherds has all the symbolic significance one can expect from what one has seen of the shepherd nature of Moses and David, mediators of the old covenant and the royal covenant, both of which Jesus would fulfill in ways no one could anticipate.[17] These also are nonetheless historiographic—because covenantal—parallels. Very shortly after this celebration, however, the young covenant mediator was subject to persecution. Herod's efforts to kill him parallel Pharaoh's efforts to kill the mediator of the old covenant. That is so even though Pharaoh's assessment of matters lacked enough

---

16. Cf. *BT* 2, 199–200; *BT* 3, 18–19.

17. Moses was a shepherd in Midian (Exod 3:1) who later shepherded God's people through the wilderness (Isa 63:11); David was a shepherd (1 Sam 17:15) who became king and thereby shepherd of God's people (2 Sam 24:17); Jesus was and remains "the good shepherd" (John 10:11).

information to target the covenant mediator specifically. The parallel is remarkable in itself—in fact, it is singular—and strongly suggests that each king was moved by spiritual forces he did not understand (in the case of Pharaoh) or credit (in the case of Herod).

CONCLUSION

The overall comparison of Exodus and the gospel genre, as illustrated by Matthew's Gospel, like the theophanic *Gattung* considered before, illustrates the same truth about biblical historiography. The literary/historiographical parallels in the Old and New Testaments occur because the Lord did similar things in similar ways in the days of the old and new covenants. In this regard, they would appear to have no indebtedness to the way the contemporaries of Moses or the Gospel writers wrote history, and it is hard to imagine how they could. No pagan historian recorded such things because they never happened in pagan contexts.

The assessment just made regarding aspects of biblical historiography does not mean that Old or New Testament writers wrote in a vacuum or totally ignored how things were written in the cultures around them. It is well known, for example, that the second millennium BC ancient Near Eastern treaty genre informs the Old Testament, that Hebrew poets used poetical forms and word pairs already well established in their day, and so on, and that, for example, New Testament epistolary style owes a debt to the way letters were written in the Greco-Roman world.

The point for the present study is this: one need not use pagan stylistic criteria as tools to categorize or understand, or qualify or disqualify, every literary device or genre we find in the Old and New Testaments. Study of biblical genres and literary devices in their own right is a legitimate undertaking, especially when they appear to have little or no indebtedness to the way the surrounding cultures wrote history.

In the following pages I address the phenomenon of laconic reporting of an event in the first instance, supplemented, I propose, by a later report that provides real and valuable information not supplied by the historian in the earlier account. If this proposal is correct, one may guess at the historian's reason for composing the history in this way, even if one cannot be sure: perhaps it was dramatic or pedagogical; perhaps it was both. All history writing would seem to be unavoidably laconic, and since the New Testament itself provides the clearest statement of this reality (cf. John 21:24–25), the proposed study will proceed both with care and with confidence that the principle of laconic reporting is well and biblically established.

Finally, although the present study is mainly historiographical, the small set of verses that form the focus of the study (Gen 2:17 and 3:2–3) affords scope for theological reflection. Theological observations and questions will appear in the course of the study with summary theological reflections in a postscript. Of primary importance will be the woman's verbal response to the serpent (Gen 3:2–3) and the effect of his words on her (Gen 3:6).

I

WHAT IS SIN, AND WHEN DID EVE DO IT?

This chapter presents an introductory discussion of the proposition that Genesis 2:17 and 3:2–3 stand in a particular historiographical relation to one another: a laconic report of an event by a third-person omniscient narrator (the historiographer, in Genesis 2), followed by a first-person retelling of the same event (also recorded by the historiographer, in Genesis 3) that adds further information not provided in the first account.

By way of a personal note on the subject, I remember years ago sitting in Meredith Kline's course Old Testament Hermeneutics at Gordon-Conwell Theological Seminary. The course never got beyond Genesis 22—despite its title, *Old Testament* Hermeneutics—but it was still a formative experience. There, I heard a new idea about Eve: that when she quoted God's prohibition from Genesis 2:17, she was *adding* to what God had said. When the serpent posed his question (Gen 3:1), she responded: "God did say, 'You must not eat fruit from the tree that is in the middle of the garden, *and you must not touch it*, or you will die'" (Gen 3:3, emphasis added). The Lord, however, had only said, "You must not eat from the tree of the knowledge of good and evil, for when you eat from it you will certainly die" (Gen 2:17). The Lord had said nothing about touching the tree. Consequently, when the woman answered the serpent, she was already starting to go astray: she added to what God had said. Even worse, she attributed words to God that God had not said.

As a young student I naturally thought my professor must be right. Only years later did the true significance of this interpretation occur to me: if the woman was adding to God's words when she answered the serpent's question she was not only *starting* to go astray, she was *already sinning*—she was saying God said what God had not said.[1] She was telling a falsehood. Even if we give her the benefit of the doubt and suppose she was only misremembering, she was *still in sin*, because she was misrepresenting what God had said. A misstatement of a fact is an *untruth* whether the misstatement is deliberate or accidental.[2]

One may also doubt the possibility that a human in an unfallen condition could "misremember" anything. We should probably be reluctant to attribute to our sinless, pre-fall parents motives or qualities that are common enough in fallen humans but would be blemishes and flaws in humans who were meant to be without fault. It might help in this regard if we consider whether Jesus—the only person without sin since the fall—could have "misremembered" something God had told him or wanted him to say because of some fault of his memory, some constitutional flaw of his nature. Jesus did say, "These words you hear are not my own; they belong to the Father who sent me" (John 14:24).

Apart from such considerations, however, it is worth noting that the Bible never faults the woman for what she says to the serpent

---

1. Regarding the woman's name: I try to avoid calling the woman "Eve" before the fall because she only receives that name after the fall. So I will refer to her henceforth in this work as "the woman," "Adam's wife," etc.

2. This may seem a very abstract or theoretical concept to many, and we will return to it for further discussion.

regarding the tree. Moreover, Paul tells us: "Adam was not the one deceived; it was the woman who was deceived and became a sinner" (1 Tim 2:14). Her sin, then, happened *after* the serpent tempted her and misled her into a *deceived condition*. But her supposedly flawed answer to the serpent came *before* the serpent's temptation. The present chapter pursues these and related issues.

BRIEF REVIEW OF THE SITUATION

Before considering the history of scholarship on the issue it may help to review from the beginning the situation under discussion. There will be more to say about this encounter in chapter 4, but for now we touch upon the main points of the woman's conversation with the serpent.

We are introduced to the serpent and advised that he was more cunning than any creature of the field the Lord had made. Next we see the serpent with the woman. He opens the conversation with an apparently harmless question: "Did God really say, 'You must not eat from any tree in the garden'?" (Gen 3:1). The question seems innocent, but it is barbed. The emphatic "did God *really* say" (אלהים אף כי אמר) lays the groundwork for further questioning of God's word. (Then the serpent misquotes God: "You must not eat from *any* tree in the garden?" The word translated "any" (כל) and, in fact, the whole phrase, "from any tree in the garden," is identical to what the Lord had told the man before: "You are free to eat from any (כל) tree in the garden" (Gen 2:16). The only difference is that the serpent has turned God's *permission* on its head, making it a *prohibition*—"You may *not* eat from any tree in the garden." He changes God's positive statement into a negative statement by adding "not." For the purposes of this discussion, changing a statement from positive to negative is quite different from adding more true information to a statement. The former contradicts the prior report. The latter shows the prior report to be laconic.

The serpent's reversal of God's statement is, apparently, meant to soften the ground for acceptance of his subsequent innuendo that God does not have human interests at heart, since it already suggests that God has denied some good things to the humans—the fruit of *any* tree in the garden.[3] The woman knows the serpent's question does not reflect the facts, but an idea may have been planted.[4]

The woman responds with a true statement: she and her husband may indeed eat from the trees in the garden (Gen 3:2). Her statement corrects the serpent's misstatement. But she says more. She conveys God's original command about the tree in the middle of the garden: "God did say, 'You must not eat fruit from the tree that is in the middle of the garden'" (Gen 3:3a), but she also says, "'and you must not touch it, or you will die'" (Gen 3:3b).[5] That latter statement has long been seen by almost all interpreters as an unwarranted addition to what God had said to Adam in Genesis 2, but it is here proposed that it would be a mistake to see her statement as an unwarranted addition. Such an addition—that is, additional words that she attributes to God even though he did not say them—would not only be a misrepresentation of what God actually said. It would be an act of *sin* on her part. Some discussion of sin and its counterpart, faith, may help show how this would be the case.

---

3. One might object that this amounts to imputing a motive to the serpent even though, as will later appear, I counsel against imputing motives to the woman. This objection has the appearance of being important. However, since we know the serpent is lying, and—to draw upon later revelation—is "a liar and the father of lies" (John 8:44), and also that he is "the tempter" (Matt 4:3), it does him no injustice to suspect him of aiming to soften up the woman's defenses, and to tempt her into taking the fruit she should not take, by posing an untruthful question.

4. Planted but—it is important to understand—not yet received by the woman as acceptable. God himself has ideas of evil, but he does not agree that they are acceptable.

5. Her variation "or you will die" is a summary statement in a summary review of Gen 2:17b ("for when you eat from it you will certainly die"). See further discussion in chapter 2.

A NOTE ON THE NATURE OF FAITH

In order to understand what was and was not sin on the woman's part—and thus to understand sin at its most fundamental level—it is important to understand faith; Paul says, "Whatever is not from faith is sin" (Rom 14:23 NKJV). I affirm Paul's statement as a categorical definition of the nature of sin. He does not list various sorts of sins and then arrive inductively at a definition of sin; he tells us what sin essentially is. Sin *is* (ἐστίν) "whatever is not from faith." Therefore, if one wants to understand the nature of sin, it would seem one must understand the nature of faith. Not everyone will agree with this approach or with the definition of faith that follows. Even so, I hope the presentation of later biblical examples similar to the Genesis 2:17/Genesis 3:3 parallel and the discussion of the laconic nature of reporting presented in chapters 2, 3, and 5 of this work will at least call into question the prevailing tradition of thought regarding the woman's response to the serpent.

The definition of faith that follows is consistent with what Paul says and with the definition presented in Hebrews 11:1. It also accords with an understanding of Genesis 15:6 advanced some years ago by Meredith Kline.[6] I have argued elsewhere that faith is the act of *amening* who God is and what he is doing.[7] Study of the Hebrew verb האמין (to believe) offers a perspective that agrees with Hebrews 11:1 and with all biblical illustrations of faith. The root of the Hebrew (Hiphil) form is the verb אמן (to confirm, support), from which the adverb אמן (amen; verily, truly) derives.[8] The basic sense, then, of the Hiphil האמן (to believe) is actually, to paraphrase, "to affirm, to

---

6. Cf. Meredith G. Kline, "Abram's *Amen*," *WTJ* 31 (1968/69): 1–11. For Kline on the delocutive nature of Abram's amen, cf. further *BT* 2, 126n36.

7. Cf. *BT* 1, 14–20; *BT* 3, appendix E.

8. Cf. Francis Brown, Samuel Rolles Driver, and Charles A. Briggs, *A Hebrew and English Lexicon of the Old Testament* (Oxford: Clarendon, 1904), 52–53.

agree that it is so."[9] That understanding would appear to convey the actual substance of biblical faith: an *agreement that something is so* in the sense that, to paraphrase, we "own" it. This act of owning something is analogous to what happens when a point made by a preacher resonates with someone in the congregation and that person cries out, "Amen—preach it!" When the hearer says "Amen," he or she is declaring ownership—a wholehearted embracing of or agreement with the point just made by the preacher.

Jesus' encounter with the centurion in Matthew 8 illustrates the same understanding of faith, as I have outlined elsewhere.[10] What Paul says in Romans 12 is entirely consistent with this view: "Do not think of yourself more highly than you ought, but rather think of yourself with sober judgment, in accordance with the faith God has distributed to each of you" (Rom 12:3). If one does not think of oneself more highly than one ought—if, consequently, one thinks of oneself as one really is or, as Paul puts it, "with sober judgment"— then one is thinking of oneself "in accordance with the faith God has distributed to each of you." It is clear from this that the apostle affirms the understanding of faith advanced here: biblical faith is seeing and embracing *God's point of view*—in this case, seeing oneself as one really is, as God sees one. It is a gift of God, who alone sees all things as they truly are. So one "amens" God and God's view of oneself, to the extent that God enables one to do so—that is, "in

---

9. Cf. William Holladay, *A Concise Hebrew and Aramaic Lexicon of the Old Testament* (Grand Rapids: Eerdmans, 1971), 20 ("view [something] as reliable, believe").

10. *BT* 1, 17. In brief: the centurion offers his job description as part of an authority structure, and then concludes that, just as he can give a command and it must be carried out, so Jesus—implicitly because he, too, is part of a similar authority structure—can just say the word, and the centurion's servant will be healed. Jesus responds in surprise that he has not found anywhere in Israel such great *faith*. In effect, the centurion intuits a truth about Jesus, and he then amens that truth, and the result is that Jesus proves his faith to be true by healing his servant with a word. By faith, the centurion could see and embrace a truth that many contemporary Israelites could not see.

accordance with the faith God has distributed to each of you." A life
of faith is consequently a life that amens God in everything. That is
a faithful life and, as such, a faultless ongoing witness to who God is
and what he is saying or doing. Only one human always lived that
way: Jesus, who is therefore called "the faithful witness" (Rev 1:5).

Nonetheless, although the second Adam was the only human
to live his whole life in such a condition until he laid down his life
(and he continues to live and be the faithful witness in heaven),
the first Adam and his wife also lived without sin until the woman
agreed with the serpent's torah and took the fruit.[11] It is important
to be clear on this matter precisely in light of the tradition that
will come under review—that is, the tradition that sees the woman
already at fault because she added to what God had said about the
tree (Gen 2:17b vis-à-vis Gen 3:3b).

CAN A SINLESS PERSON
"MISREMEMBER"?

Some interpreters think the woman may have "misremembered"
what the Lord had said. That proposal seems problematic: How
can a flawless person misremember something? But behind that
problem stands a prior problem, which has to do with the nature of
Adam's report to his wife when he told her what the Lord had said.
It is assumed here that Adam told his wife exactly what the Lord
had said. If Adam had not told her exactly what the Lord said, Adam
himself was at fault for either (1) lying to his wife deliberately for
whatever reason, or (2) himself misremembering what the Lord had
said. Scripture does not say Adam lied to his wife about what the
Lord said. Had he done so, he would already have been a sinner. On

---

11. Cf. also the important idiom used mostly in covenantal contexts, שמע לקול,
in Gen 3:17, and discussion in *BT* 1, 113–15. The Hebrew term *torah*, which means
"law, instruction," is used in the OT both for the Mosaic law and for any particular
law or instruction.

the other hand, if Adam was the one who misremembered what the Lord had said, the interpreter's task at this point would remain the same: to explore the proposal that a person who was in an unfallen condition could misremember something.

Two possible ways of accounting for such an event are: (1) God did not create humans with a perfect ability to remember, or (2) God did create humans with a perfect ability to remember, but they could misremember if some cause for doing so arose within them. The second possibility involves something we know to be true: God created humans who, although without sin, were nonetheless able to sin.

What about the first possibility—namely, that God did not create humans with a perfect ability to remember? Are there biblical data that enable one to answer this question—or at least to propose an answer that is so likely to be correct that one can consider the question to be answered in the most likely way? Two answers based on biblical data readily present themselves.

The first answer is expressed in one biblical datum: God declared that everything he had created was "very good" (Gen 1:31). Arguably, the biblical concept of what is "good" is aligned with the biblical concept of what is righteous. Jesus says, "There is only One who is good" (Matt 19:17). He includes himself, of course, in an ironic reply to the man who asks him what good thing he must do to inherit eternal life (Matt 19:16). Nonetheless, that God is good is important, for God is also righteous. As I have argued elsewhere, biblical righteousness is conformity to the standard of God, and God's own righteousness is his conformity to the standard of himself—God is always true to himself.[12] Jesus is "Jesus Christ the righteous" because he always conformed and does conform to the standard of his Father's nature.

---

12. *BT* 3, appendix E.

To be "good" and to be "righteous" are two sides of the same coin.[13]
If for the sake of argument one allows this concise assessment, it
follows that before the fall God could say that everything he had
created was "good," meaning that it was consistent with God's nature
and it was just what God wanted it to be.[14] That "all" in Genesis 1:31
included Adam and his wife before the fall. Adam and his wife
before the fall, then, were "good." They were also righteous: they
conformed to God's nature in every respect that, on the creaturely
level, they should. On the spiritual level, they were without sin—
they were amening God in everything they thought, said, and did.
On the physical level they were flawless—they did not suffer from
any impairment of vision, hearing, speech, organs, or mental ability,
including the ability to remember things.

The second response to the question, "Did God, or did he not,
create humans with a perfect ability to remember?" lies more in
the moral or ethical sphere as it pertains to God himself. If God
did create humans with a perfect ability to remember things, then
the moral failure of Adam's wife, or of Adam himself, cannot lie in
their failure to remember accurately what the Lord had said. On
the other hand, if God did *not* create them with a perfect ability to
remember things, then he created them with a serious defect. If
they could fail to remember things accurately, they could potentially misremember all sorts of things that would become important if they were to carry out the "cultural mandate" (i.e., Gen 1:28)
successfully. More dreadfully, if they could fail to remember things

---

13. Cf. the claim, "The Lᴏʀᴅ is *good* [טוב] and his love endures forever; / his *faithfulness* [אמונתו] continues through all generations" (Ps 100:5, emphases added). The
Lord's "faithfulness" includes his righteousness—i.e., his faithfulness to himself—
and this is paralleled with his being "good." Cf. Jesus' statement paralleling "good"
and "righteous" (in chiasmus, Matt 5:45), and also Paul's statement that parallels
"righteous" and "good": "Very rarely will anyone die for a righteous person, though
for a good person someone might possibly dare to die" (Rom 5:7).

14. Cf. related affirmations in Ps 19:1–4; Rom 1:20.

accurately, they could misremember the all-important injunction of Genesis 2:17b with disastrous consequences. We know God does not want "anyone to perish" (2 Pet 3:9). If what Peter wrote is true of God after the fall, would it not have been true of God before the fall? I therefore consider it unlikely that God created the first man and woman with a defect—that is, with a flawed ability to remember things.

Finally, it is important to stress that the issue is their *ability* to remember. Since they were obviously capable of sinning, they were also capable of distorting their memory out of some sinful motive that arose within them. On that understanding, however, if either Adam misremembered what God had said or his wife misremembered what Adam had said that God had said, their distorted recollections would have arisen out of sinful motives, and they would already have been in sin before the woman took the fruit. I here propose, then, that God did not create them with defective memories that could almost guarantee their fall, but he did create them with the ability to choose sin.

DETERMINATION OF EVIDENCE: A METHODOLOGICAL EXCURSUS ON BONHOEFFER AND BARTH

What evidence should contribute to an analysis of the events of Genesis 2 and 3? Presumably, one should take as evidence the data those passages provide along with any relevant New Testament data. The history of interpretation, however, offers many examples of articulate and persuasive analyses that appear to depart from the limited evidence the Bible provides. Moreover, commentators ancient and modern have not considered the historiographical aspect of the apparent contrast between Genesis 2:17 and Genesis 3:2–3 by comparing them with potentially analogous examples of historiography elsewhere in the Bible.

This omission may seem surprising, but trying to explain how this could be seems fairly pointless. The way one interprets a passage has roots in one's training and experience. A scholar who grew up in a harshly fundamentalist household may in reaction take a very critical and even destructive view of the authenticity of the Bible.[15] A scholar whose theological education took place in a higher critical context may have a very skeptical view of the historicity of the Old Testament (or parts of it) even if that same scholar has put his faith in Christ. But if one abandons the historicity of biblical history, one abandons the factual anchor of exegesis. Subjectivity will then reign.[16] Two well-known theologians are worth considering in this regard: Dietrich Bonhoeffer and Karl Barth, contemporaries in the world of German and Old Testament scholarship and theology, show how the sort of subjectivity we are discussing can produce diametrically opposite results. Their contrary interpretations of the Eden narratives (Genesis 2 and 3) are cases in point.

---

15. The history of modern biblical scholarship has a number of such cases, and there is no need, or perhaps even appropriateness, in mentioning any scholar by name as an illustration.

16. This affirmation about historicity must naturally be qualified with regard to Gen 1:1–2:3 because the genres involved suggest that although the passage presents historical realities (i.e., God did in fact create everything, and in a principled way that reflects his own character), it presents them in such a way as to schematize both the covenantal nature of the relationships involved (i.e., God created everything, including the first man and woman, in a type of relationship with himself that would later be called covenantal) and in such a way as to illustrate the principle of authority that pervades the created order (i.e., the "Framework Hypothesis" developed in its most mature form by Meredith Kline). In other words, Gen 1:1–2:3 presents historical realities but not in the simple, straightforward chronological narrative that one typically envisions when one thinks of written history. It is historical reality, but it is more than that. See the discussion in *BT* 1, chapter 1; *BT* 2, 6–11.

TWO EXAMPLES

Dietrich Bonhoeffer

Dietrich Bonhoeffer, a famous and highly regarded theologian who struggled to affirm Christian faith in the face of the Nazi regime, wrote valuable works that make important points for Christians (perhaps most famously the importance of not dispensing "cheap grace"). That he had a true faith may be surprising to some, considering the intellectual and theological climate in which he was educated. The world of Old Testament scholarship that helped form Bonhoeffer's view of Genesis was the result of over a century of German liberal scholarship. The best scholarship of his day thought the early chapters of Genesis were mythological, and—if "historical" at all—historical only in a very qualified sense.

Bonhoeffer believed that higher criticism provided the scientific background for the study of Genesis. That view was prevalent in the early twentieth century and is still very common today.[17] As a result he could view the account of the garden and humans in it before the fall both as mythological and as historical truth ("an event at the beginning of history, before history, beyond history, and yet in history") affirmed by the church.[18]

---

17. Dietrich Bonhoeffer, *Creation and Fall*, in *The Bonhoeffer Reader*, ed. Clifford J. Green and Michael P. DeJonge (Minneapolis: Fortress, 2013), 244, states, for example, "The Yahwist too was a human being in the middle. Only in this way is it possible to lay all the guilt on human beings and at the same time to express how inconceivable, inexplicable, and inexcusable that guilt is."

18. Bonhoeffer, *Creation and Fall*, 230; considering the account as myth (according to the world) and as history (according to the church), he says, "Why contend for one assertion at the expense of the other? Why not see that all our speaking of God, of our beginning and end, and of our guilt *never* communicates these things themselves but always only pictures of them?" And again, "The exposition of what follows must therefore seek to translate the old picture language of the magical world into the new picture language of the technical world."

If one views the early materials of Genesis as myth, or magical pictures, and not exclusively as history in the literal sense (however laconically reported), one already encounters problems arriving at a realistic view of the material. Interpretation becomes largely subjective. It may be no surprise, then, that Bonhoeffer comes up with some bizarre statements about the accounts in Genesis 2 and Genesis 3—statements that unfortunately find little support in the narratives. His comments on what Adam could not have known, when the Lord told him not to eat of the tree of the knowledge of good and evil or he would surely die, are a good example:

> How is Adam to grasp what death is, what good and evil are, indeed even what a prohibition is, living as Adam does in unbroken obedience to the Creator? Can any of this mean anything else than empty words to Adam? Certainly Adam cannot know what death is, what good and evil are; but Adam understands that in these words God confronts Adam and points out Adam's limit.[19]

"Certainly Adam cannot know what death is, what good and evil are." Adam cannot even grasp "what a prohibition is." These statements raise questions of evidence—questions that will be cardinal in the discussion of Genesis 2 and 3. What is the evidentiary basis for Bonhoeffer's statements?

To address the question of death and Adam's knowledge of it: a traditional view has been that Adam would have seen death even as he took and ate fruit, which begins to die when it is plucked and does die when it is consumed. Apart from such a reply, which one would probably have to say is speculative, the fact would appear to be that a person today can have no sure way of knowing what

---

19. Bonhoeffer, *Creation and Fall*, 232. He affirms that the prohibition does communicate to Adam his limitedness, his creatureliness.

Adam could or could not know about death, or about good and evil, because Genesis 2 does not provide that information. One principle that will appear again and again in the present work is this: the narrative accounts of the Bible are laconic. Consequently, it would appear to be unrealistic to assert what may or may not have been the case ("Certainly Adam cannot know") when the Bible does not establish the matter as a fact. We know some things the Lord said to Adam. We cannot know what else the Lord may have communicated to Adam about the tree of knowledge of good and evil or about death. Moreover if, as Bonhoeffer says, God's injunction pointed out to Adam his "limit," that ipso facto makes it clear "what a prohibition is": it is a statement that sets a limit to what one may be or do. Furthermore, what does it say about God as Adam's loving creator, if he tells Adam something of importance that can only be "empty words" to Adam?[20] One might at least hope the Lord would be a better communicator. When the Lord told Adam he must "not" eat the fruit of the tree of the knowledge of good and evil, there is no evidence that God used words that Adam could not understand. The Lord's later rebuke to Adam ("Have you eaten from the tree that I commanded you not to eat from?"; Gen 3:11) seems to assume that Adam was responsible for understanding and obeying God's command.[21] The fact that Adam was at that point "living ... in unbroken obedience to the Creator" does not ipso facto mean such words from the Lord must be "empty words to Adam." The conclusion would seem to be a non sequitur. It could be that a state of sinless and unbroken obedience to God means one could not know what death was, or what a prohibition was, but to say so goes beyond the

---

20. Something, we might add, of life-or-death importance for Adam.

21. The covenant lawsuit interrogation of Gen 3:11 would be without merit if the command that was broken had been impossible to understand. God's justice then would have been the rawest case of justice as "the will of the stronger"—a characterization contrary to everything the Bible tells us about God.

evidence.[22] Bonhoeffer has presented as facts what, unfortunately, cannot be established from the laconic information provided by the narrative.

Karl Barth

Karl Barth produced, in his *Church Dogmatics*, an interpretation of Adam's condition in Eden that is the very opposite of the one Bonhoeffer offered, notwithstanding that both theologians took a higher-critical view of Genesis. In Barth's view, Adam—far from not understanding or being unable to know what God had told him—not only understood what God had said but took it upon himself to wage war against sin in the form of the serpent-injunction complex. Barth's understanding of Adam's transgression regarding the tree of knowledge of good and evil is worth exploring in its own right, the more so because the events in Eden are of a primordial and foundational nature. The nature of sin thus becomes an important question from Genesis 2 onward, and it just has been discussed in relation to faith. Barth, however, defines sin not as whatever "is not from faith" (per Rom 14:23) but as the "concrete form of nothingness," a concept that must be assumed without lengthy discussion at this point.[23] Barth's understanding of sin conditions his understanding of Adam's transgression. If sin is the "concrete form of nothingness," it stands to reason that combating sin is beyond the capacity of a human, for who can come to grips with "nothingness"? So it is for Adam. For Barth, it is beyond the power of the human creature both to confront and defeat sin:

---

22. Incidentally but not insignificantly, since the prohibition defined a type of disobedience that was proscribed, it thereby also defined something that was evil: disobedience to God. It would follow that Adam could know at least one thing that was evil, without gaining the sort of "knowledge" of evil that he could obtain by eating the forbidden fruit.

23. For discussion and interaction, cf. *BT* 3, chapter 4.

In face of real nothingness the creature is already defeated
and lost. For, as Gen 3 shows, it regards the conflict with it
as its own cause, and tries to champion it as such. It tries to
be itself the hero who suffers and fights and conquers, *and
therefore like God*. And because this decision is a decision
against the grace of God, it is a choice of evil. For good—the
one and only good of the creature—is the free grace of God,
the action of his mercy, in which He who has no need to
do so has made the controversy with nothingness His own,
exposing Himself to its attack and undertaking to repel it.[24]

Barth's explanation of the man and woman's transgression in
Genesis 3 appears, unfortunately, to go far beyond the information
Genesis 3 provides. A natural reading of Genesis 3 understands
that our first parents succumbed to the temptation to be *omniscient*,
like God/the heavenly beings.[25] They were—being without sin—
perfectly able to say no to the temptation. The human creatures
could have been victorious over sin. Instead they gave in to it, and
so they gave the serpent/Satan and his angels legal entrée into the
world and made him the "god of this age" (2 Cor 4:4).[26] The text of
Genesis 3 does not present us with a woman or a man who takes
it upon herself or himself to do battle with nothingness or with its
concrete form of sin as presented in the person of the serpent. That

24. Karl Barth, *Church Dogmatics* III, 3: *The Doctrine of Creation*, trans. G. W.
Bromiley and R. J. Ehrlich (Edinburgh: T&T Clark, 1960), 413, emphasis added; cf.
Karl Barth, *Kirchliche Dogmatik* III, 3: *Die Lehre von der Schöpfung* (Zollikon-Zürich:
Evangelischer Verlag A.G., 1950), 358. The English and German versions are hence-
forth referenced as *CD* and *KD* respectively. Cf. discussion and German text in
Niehaus, *BT* 3, 132–36 (including discussion of Barth on Gen 1:2 and its supposed
mythological background).

25. For the ambiguous understanding of אלהים as "God/the heavenly beings" in
Gen 3:5, see Niehaus, *BT* 1, 98–99.

26. Niehaus, *BT* 1, 112.

was apparently not the way in which—as Barth would have it—they sought to become "like God."

It should also be noted that Barth comes close to Augustine when he characterizes nothingness as privation.[27] Evil in the Christian sense, he says, is alien and adverse to grace and therefore without grace: "In this sense nothingness is really privation [*Eben in diesem Sinne ist das Nichtige wirklich Privation*]," the attempt to defraud both God and his creature of salvation and right.[28]

Quite apart from Barth's understanding of sin, which seems to have been laudably motivated to avoid making God the author of sin, what stands out is Barth's portrayal of Adam and the way in which Adam tried to be like God. It is hard to find a foundation for such an interpretation in Genesis 3 itself. Genesis 2:17b does not define sin qua sin. It does prohibit one type of sinful act: eating from the tree of the knowledge of good and evil. It would seem impossible to arrive exegetically (on such a basis) at the interpretation Barth reaches about Adam's sin: that the human creature "tries to be itself the hero who suffers and fights and conquers, *and therefore like God.*"

DETERMINATION OF EVIDENCE AND THE PRESENT WORK

Bonhoeffer and Barth have presented two radically different views of Eden before the fall. Nonetheless, their explanations have two very important things in common: (1) both proceed from a higher-critical perspective, and (2) both attribute to Adam mental states—psychological states and states of knowledge—that are not presented as such anywhere in the text. The higher-critical perspective that they shared, which discounts the historicity of the material, may

---

27. See Niehaus, *BT* 3, 121–23, for discussion of Augustine's understanding of sin—an early contribution to the theological tradition in which Barth stands on this matter.

28. Barth, *CD*, 353; Barth, *KD*, 408.

have given them opportunity to treat the material so freely. In any case, the way of interpreting the material that they model—which is actually eisegetical—is unfortunately more common than one would hope in treatments of Genesis 2 and 3.

The following review will indicate that most interpretations of the issue at hand (the relationship of Genesis 2:17 and Genesis 3:2–3) are characterized by one or both of two tendencies. First, and regrettably, eisegesis is a common factor in the interpretations that have addressed the woman's reply to the serpent and also in analyses of what transpired in the Genesis 2 background to her response. A second problem is the prevalent tendency to psychoanalyze the woman on the basis of her statement in Genesis 3:3b in an effort to explain the particulars of her path toward taking and eating the fruit. Bonhoeffer may actually offer one of the more attractive examples of such analysis, and it is quoted now—both for its merit and for the problem it raises—as a bridge to the following chapter:

> The possibility of our *own* "will to be for God," discovered by ourselves, is the real evil in the serpent's question. It is not a piece of stupidity, it is the very summit of the serpent's cunning that it exaggerates so grossly in this question, "*Did God say, you shall not eat of any tree in the garden?*" With this it has Eve on its side from the very first, indeed, it compels her to the confession, No naturally God did not say that. The fact that Eve must qualify something regarding a Word of God—even if it is falsely represented—must throw her into the greatest confusion. It must indeed enable her to feel, for the first time, the attraction of making judgments about the Word of God. By means of the obviously false the serpent will now bring down that which is right.[29]

---

29. Dietrich Bonhoeffer, *Creation and Fall: A Theological Interpretation of Genesis 1–3*, in *Creation and Fall & Temptation: Two Biblical Studies*, trans. John C. Fletcher (New York: Macmillan, 1963), 68.

Bonhoeffer's idea of "our *own* 'will to be for God,' discovered by ourselves," appears to show an essential understanding of sin. Self-will, even aiming to do what we think God wants us to do or something favorable to God, is actually, as a self-generated act apart from God's will, sin. To employ the term used above, it does not amen God. It decides what would be good for God, or for his cause, and then tries to do it. Our self-will is conveyed into action. This may explain what Barth meant when he characterized Adam's sin as the moment and the action when the creature "regards the conflict with it [i.e., with sin, or "nothingness," *das Nichtige*] as its own cause, and tries to champion it as such. It tries to be itself the hero who suffers and fights and conquers, *and therefore like God*. And because this decision is a decision against the grace of God, it is a choice of evil."[30] Barth's analysis does, however, appear to neglect the point that the Lord put Adam into the garden "to work and to *take care of/keep/guard* it" (Gen 2:15). It was in fact Adam's *job* to conflict with and ward off any evil—notwithstanding that there is no evidence that Adam knew of any evil in the garden before his wife offered him the fruit.[31] On the other hand, had Adam assumed any responsibility or done any act that was not amening the Lord, that would have been sin.

The latter possibility seems to be the one Bonhoeffer has in mind, though he does not express it in the same terms. His idea of "our *own* 'will to be for God,' discovered by ourselves," shows an essential understanding of sin, as has been noted. However, the

---

30. Barth, *CD*, 413; Barth, *KD*, 358.

31. Related to this point, there is no unambiguous evidence that Adam was "with" his wife at the moment she was tempted, despite the tendency in some translations to suggest that she was—see ESV, NIV, HCSB. Cf. discussion of the Hebrew of Gen 3:6b in Niehaus, *BT* I, 100–102.

biblical passage shows no sign that the woman is thinking that way when she answers the serpent's question.[32]

The more attractive point of psychological insight in Bonhoeffer's reasoning may be this: "The fact that Eve must qualify something regarding a Word of God—even if it is falsely represented ... must indeed enable her to feel, for the first time, the attraction of making judgments about the Word of God." This may or may not be. We are not told by the omniscient narrator that such is the case—that the woman begins to feel herself as a judge of the word of God or begins to feel the attractiveness of making judgments about the word of God. She is simply presented as someone who says what (according to her at least) God said. The argument of the present work is that she is repeating to the serpent the fuller version of what the Lord had said to Adam (which was laconically reported). Whatever the progress of her state of mind, it is tragically true that she chose to accept the *serpent's* word—*his* torah—rather than the Lord's. That is clear because she acted on what the serpent told her (Gen 3:6).

Attractive therefore as Bonhoeffer's psychological portrayal of the woman may be at this point—and however much it may resonate with one's understanding of one's own, fallen mental processes—wisdom rests with discretion. It would be better not to impute to the woman any thoughts the text does not unambiguously show us to be true.

Interpretations of the woman's temptation and fall now come up for review. As noted, the study will encounter two difficulties that have been characteristic of most interpretations: (1) eisegesis with regard to various unreported details and/or acts, and (2) a prevalent tendency to psychoanalyze the woman (on the basis of her statement in Genesis 3:3b) in an effort to explain the particulars of her path toward taking and eating the fruit. The second problem

---

32. As discussion in the following chapters hopes to show.

also falls under the umbrella of eisegesis, but it deserves recognition in its own right because of its unique importance when one comes to the question of evidence regarding the woman's behavior and motives.

2

HISTORY OF INTERPRETATION: JEWISH AND EARLY CHRISTIAN

Chapters 2 and 3 are devoted to the history of interpretation. The history is well populated and deserves consideration because it shows how individual scholars repeat and nuance long-held views. Some of their speculations even have entertainment value. They are also cautionary examples of how far speculation can go.

A sampling of Jewish and early Christian interpreters shows at least two things. One, the early interpreters imagined the same possibilities as the majority of later, Reformation and post-Reformation interpreters: (a) either the woman added Genesis 3:3b to what God had said in Genesis 2:17b, or (b) Adam told his wife the wrong thing, which she then repeated to the serpent. Two, the early interpreters indulged their imaginations with some freedom. In particular, they were much more eisegetical than later interpreters. Before reviewing their commentaries, a précis of Genesis 3:1–3 can set the scene. The review in this chapter and the next will form the background for a presentation of evidence for the point of view advocated in this work—namely, that the woman did not add to what God had told Adam, but rather, she supplemented the laconic reporting of Genesis 2:17. The evidence will include parallel examples from Genesis. Chapter 5 will include what may be parallel historiographical cases from Acts.

BRIEF REVIEW OF GENESIS 3:1–3:
WHO SAID WHAT

When the serpent asks the woman if she and her husband may not eat from any tree in the garden, she answers, "We may eat fruit from the trees in the garden, but God did say, 'You must not eat fruit from the tree that is in the middle of the garden, and you must not touch it, or you will die'" (literally, "lest you die"; Gen 3:2b–3).[1] Why does Adam's wife give that answer? Interpreters have offered two possibilities. One is Adam told her exactly what God had said, but she adds to it. This has been the majority view. Another view is Adam did not tell her exactly what God had said; rather, Adam himself added the proviso, "and you shall not touch it." As was noted in chapter 1, the second view conceals an insurmountable problem, because it attributes sin to Adam before the fall. Nonetheless it is a very old view.

JEWISH INTERPRETERS

PHILO

The Jewish philosopher Philo of Alexandria (c. 25 BC–c. AD 50) thought the woman added to what the Lord had said:

> Why, when the command was given not to eat of one particular tree, did the woman include even approaching it closely,

---

1. The serpent uses the plural verb, "you may not eat." He thereby evokes the fact that God's injunction applies to both the woman and her husband. He may also be preparing the way for the temptation he will soon lodge—by which he hopes to implicate both of the humans in sin—since the verbs and pronoun in Gen 3:4–5 are also in the plural: "You [pl.] will not certainly die. ... When you [pl.] eat from it your [pl.] eyes will be opened [pl.], and you will be [pl.] like God, knowing [pl. ptc.] good and evil." Cf. *BT* 1, 96–99.

saying, "He said, You shall not eat of that one and not come near it"?

First, because taste and every sense consists generically in its contact. Second, for the severe punishment of those who have practiced this. For if merely approaching was forbidden, would not those who, besides touching the tree, also ate of it and enjoyed it, adding a great wrong to a lesser one, become condemners and punishers of themselves?[2]

The first observation, which relates "taste and every sense" to "contact," is not germane to the present discussion because it is a philosophical observation regarding epistemology in general and does not deal with the sin issue at hand. The second observation bears on the point under consideration.

Philo reasoned according to a rabbinical interpretive criterion called *qal wahomer* ("light and heavy"), which considers, first, a "light" (Heb. *qal*) case and what its rationale(s) or consequence(s) might be and then compares a "heavy" (Heb. *homer*) case, whose rationale(s) and consequence(s) would be greater, or "heavier." Paul uses the same technique when he comments on the "heaviness" (i.e., weightiness, significance) of Christ's death (Rom 5:7–8 NKJV):

| LIGHT CASE | For scarcely for a righteous man will one die; yet perhaps for a good man someone would even dare to die. |
| HEAVY CASE | But God demonstrates His own love toward us, in that while we were still sinners, Christ died for us. |

---

2. Philo, *Questions and Answers on Genesis*, trans. Ralph Marcus, Loeb Classical Library 380 (Cambridge: Harvard University Press, 1953), 21.

One might choose to die for a good man, and that is the relatively "light" case. But one would find it much harder to die for a sinful man, so that would be the "heavy" case. This is not to say that it is a "light" matter to choose to die for anyone, but Paul's illustration makes the point: Christ did a "heavy"—i.e., very weighty and significant—thing, when he chose to lay down his life for sinful human beings.

Philo's comparison is the same (*qal wahomer*):

| LIGHT CASE | Touching the tree |
| HEAVY CASE | Eating of the tree |

Philo's logic is unassailable. However, he evidently neglected to note that when the woman added to what God had said, she was already committing a wrong. If she did create a *qal wahomer* argument, she sinned by doing so since in order to do so she had to add to what God had said. Philo, then, did not take into account the nature of sin (namely, "whatever is not of faith," whatever is not amening God; Rom 14:23 NKJV). Had he done so, he would have had to make a very different argument.

RABBI NATHAN: ADAM DID NOT TELL HIS WIFE THE TRUTH

The view that Adam did not tell his wife exactly what God had said is another view that appears among Jewish interpreters. The following evaluation appears in *The Fathers according to R. Nathan* (ca. AD 700–900):

> The text says, "And God commanded Adam, saying, 'Of the tree of the knowledge of good and evil you shall not eat, for in the day that you eat of it you shall die' [Gen 2:17]." But Adam did not choose to tell God's words to Eve exactly as

they had been spoken. Instead he said to her, "God said, 'You shall not eat of the fruit of the tree which is in the middle of the garden, neither shall you touch it, lest you die' [as per Gen 3:3]." Whereupon the wicked serpent said to himself, "Since I seem to be unable to trip up Adam, let me go and try to trip up Eve." He went and sat down next to her and started talking with her. He said: "Now you say that God has forbidden us to touch the tree. Well, I can touch the tree and not die, and so can you." What did the wicked serpent then do? He touched the tree with his hands and feet and shook it so hard that some of its fruit fell to the ground. ... Then he said to her "[You see? So likewise] you say that God has forbidden us to eat from the tree. But I can eat from it and not die, and so can you." What did Eve think to herself? "All the things that my husband has told me are lies." ... Whereupon she took the fruit and ate it and gave to Adam and he ate, as it is written, "The woman saw that the tree was good to eat from and a delight to the eyes" [Gen 3:6].[3]

Rabbi Nathan added some ingenious touches in his portrayal of what happened. The serpent tries his wiles on Adam first but fails, so he turns his attention to the woman, thinking perhaps he may be able to seduce her. He takes an experimental approach. He has hands and feet and uses them to grab and shake the tree until some of its fruit drops.[4] His experiment provides obvious proof that

---

3. 'Abot de R. Nathan A.1, as quoted in James L. Kugel, *The Bible as It Was* (Cambridge: Harvard University Press, 1997), 77. For discussion of the texts of 'Abot de R. Nathan (i.e., *The Fathers according to R. Nathan*), see Kugel, *The Bible as It Was*, 567 ("Texts and Sources"). Elements of R. Nathan's commentary have antecedents in Judaism, as noted below.

4. For the idea that the serpent had feet, see Jacob Neusner, *Genesis Rabbah: The Judaic Commentary to the Book of Genesis: A New American Translation*, vol. 1 (Atlanta: Scholars Press, 1985), 200, where Rabbi Hoshiah the Elder observes, "He stood erect

one can touch the tree and not die. The natural conclusion for the woman is then, "All the things that my husband has told me are lies." The corollary is also clear: if one can touch the tree and not die, one can also eat the fruit of the tree and not die.[5] So she does eat; but, of course, she would now also die. According to this interpretation, Adam, not his wife, originally added the words "neither shall you touch it, lest you die" to what God had said. But this cannot be the case. If Adam added the words, the same criterion must be applied to him as would be applied to the woman had she been the one who originally added to God's word: anyone who adds to what God has said is attributing words to God that he did not say. That is a lie, and of course that is a sin. One may note the Lord's warning at the end of the Bible's final book: "I warn everyone who hears the words of the prophecy of this scroll: If anyone adds anything to them, God will add to that person the plagues described in this scroll. And if anyone takes words away from this scroll of prophecy, God will take away from that person any share in the tree of life and in the Holy City, which are described in this scroll" (Rev 22:18–19). The same principle appears early: "Do not add to what I command you and do not subtract from it, but keep the commands of the LORD your God that I give you" (Deut 4:2); "See that you do all I command you; do not add to it or take away from it" (Deut 12:32). The warning applies

---

like a reed and had feet. [That is what indicated his intelligence.]," and Rabbi Simeon b. Eleazar (disciple of Rabbi Meir, AD 139–163) states, "He was like a camel. This world lost out on a great benefit, for if things had not happened the way they did, a man could send commerce through [a snake], who would come and go [doing his employer's business]."

5. Rabbi Hiyya (AD 180–230) had taught earlier, "So the Holy One, blessed be he, had said, 'For on the day on which you eat from it, you shall surely die' (Gen. 2:17). But that is not what she then said to the snake. Rather: 'God said, "You shall not eat from it *and you shall not touch it.*"' When the snake saw that she was lying to him, he took her and pushed her against the tree. He said to her, 'Have you now died? Just as you did not die for touching it, so you will not die from eating it.' Rather: 'For God knows that when you eat of it, your eyes will be opened and you will be like God (Gen. 3:5).'" See Neusner, *Genesis Rabbah*, 201–2.

in principle to any alterations made by humans to God's word(s): all such additions, subtractions or other alterations are sin because they attribute to God things he did not say, delete from the record things he did say, or diminish the accuracy of the report of what he said.[6] Jewish interpreters did recognize this principle. As will be noted later, the Babylonian Talmud teaches, "Anyone who adds subtracts." It should be added that any such alterations, whether made by Adam's wife or anyone else, are sin, even if they have not yet been defined as such at a given stage of God's revelation (cf. Rom 5:12–14; 7:10–13).

But why did Adam not tell his wife the truth, or the whole truth? A more recent exponent of the view, Rabbi Meir Zlotowitz, explains: "The woman did not describe it as a 'tree of knowledge of good and bad' because Adam probably never told her of the tree's special characteristic for he was apprehensive that if he told her she would crave to eat of it."[7] The rabbi's answer is thoughtful, but it raises questions of its own. In addition to the sin problem it implies (as discussed above), it seems reasonable to pose the question: Why should one expect Adam or his wife before the fall to have the sort of suspicions and subterfuges that occur to our fallen and corrupted natures? Is there evidence in Genesis 1–2 to support or imply that he would have such suspicions? Those chapters do not appear to offer evidence along those lines.

Modesty will be a good guide as we consider the background of scholarship regarding Genesis 2:2–3 in this and the following chapter. Another guide will be the understanding of faith presented in chapter 1.

---

6. I affirm a difference between alterations of fact and paraphrases that do not alter fact; see further discussion in chapter 3.

7. Meir Zlotowitz, *Bereishis/Genesis: A New Translation with a Commentary from Talmudic, Midrashic and Rabbinic Sources* (Brooklyn: Mesorah Publications, 1977), 116.

THE BABYLONIAN TALMUD: ADAM DID TELL
HIS WIFE THE TRUTH, BUT THE WOMAN
ADDED TO WHAT GOD HAD SAID

Did the woman in fact add to what God said? Many commentators in the history of scholarship have taken the view that the woman added to what God had said when she answered the serpent's opening question. This has been the view of most Jewish scholars.

However, as in the commentary by Rabbi Nathan just considered, the older Jewish interpreters also took what modern interpreters would consider unwarranted liberties with the text. Among Jewish commentaries, the Babylonian Talmud (ca. third to fifth centuries AD) tells us:

> **From where** is it derived **that anyone who adds, subtracts?**
> It is derived from a verse, **as it is stated** that Eve said: **"God has said: You shall not eat of it, neither shall you touch it"** (**Genesis 3:3**), whereas God had actually rendered prohibited only eating from the tree but not touching it, as it is stated: "But of the Tree of Knowledge of good and evil, you shall not eat of it" (**Genesis 2:17**). Because Eve added that there was a prohibition against touching the tree, the snake showed her that touching it does not cause her to die, and she consequently sinned by eating from it as well.[8]

Concerning which Rashi comments, "And you shall not touch it; She added to the command; therefore she came to diminish it. That is what is stated (Prov 30:6): 'Do not add to His words.'"[9] The Talmudic commentary may be seen to recognize the woman's

---

8. Sanhedrin 29a, emphasis original; https://www.sefaria.org/william-davidson-talmud.

9. Sanhedrin 29a. Cf. Neusner, *Genesis Rabbah*, 201: "It is that one should not make the fence taller than the foundation, so that the fence will not fall down and wipe out the plants" (R. Hiyya).

addition as sin, since it says, "She consequently sinned by eating from it as well." This statement could mean that she sinned by adding to what God said and then also ("as well") sinned by eating from the tree, or it could mean that she added to what God had said but then also ("as well") *sinned* by eating from it.

UMBERTO CASSUTO: THE WOMAN ADDED TO WHAT GOD HAD SAID, BUT THAT'S NOT A PROBLEM

A well-known modern Jewish scholar, Umberto Cassuto, continues in the tradition of older Jewish interpreters but with a slight difference. He thinks the woman added the words in question, but he does not see her addition as a problem:

> This ["neither shall you touch it"] is not stated in the instruc-
> tion of the Lord God quoted above (ii 17). Most exegetes,
> whether of the middle ages or contemporary, consider that
> the woman added this point of her own accord, and they
> advance various reasons for this interpretation. Jacob, in
> his commentary, suggests that Scripture purports to tell us
> here something that was actually said by the Lord God but
> was not expressly mentioned above. But this hypothesis is
> improbable, for the exact nature of the prohibition should
> have been precisely formulated when the Lord God spoke to
> the man. A more correct approach is to pay attention to the
> fact that the verb נָגַע *nāgha'* often has a graver connotation
> than mere touching, as, for example, in the following verses:
> *therefore I did not let you touch her* (xx 6); *whoever touches this*
> *man or his wife shall be put to death* (xxvi 11). Hence, in the final
> analysis the clause *neither shall you touch it* is simply syn-
> onymous with the preceding clause *you shall not eat thereof*.[10]

---

10. Umberto Cassuto, *A Commentary on the Book of Genesis, Part One: From Adam to Noah, Gen I–VI 8*, trans. Israel Abrahams (Jerusalem: Magnes, 1961), 145. Cf. Benno

Cassuto considers it improbable that "Scripture purports to tell us here something that was actually said by the Lord God but was not expressly mentioned above," for "the exact nature of the prohibition should have been precisely formulated when the Lord God spoke to the man." This view may not, however, take seriously enough the possibility that the narrative in Genesis 2:17 is laconic. The purpose of the present work is to show the relevance of that idea to Genesis 3:3b. To do so will require consideration of other parallel accounts of statements by people and by the Lord himself, in Genesis and beyond. Such a view, if correct, would mean that the "exact nature of the prohibition" was in fact "precisely formulated by the Lord God" when he spoke to Adam but not fully reported in Genesis 2.

If Cassuto's first argument regarding the woman's supposed addition seems to make her guilty of adding to what the Lord had said, his second argument appears to remove her guilt. He argues that the verb used in her addition (נגע, "to touch") can imply much more than mere touch. His two examples, one from Genesis 20:6 (the Lord did not let Abimelek "touch" Sarah—i.e., engage her sexually) and Genesis 26:11 (Abimelek gives orders regarding Isaac: "Anyone who harms [נגע, 'touches'] this man or his wife shall surely be put to death"), are truly cases in which more than mere touch is implied. English offers a similar usage—"Don't lay a hand on him/her." However, in both of the cases Cassuto chose to illustrate the idea, touching is still involved—touching with a purpose or to facilitate the advance of a purpose. Accordingly, the Lord may have commanded Adam and his wife not to "touch" the tree (note it is the *tree* and not yet the fruit itself) as well as not to eat its fruit.

Jacob, *Das erste Buch der Tora, Genesis. Übersetzt und erklärt* (Berlin: Schocken, 1934); English translation by Ernest I. Jacob and Walter Jacob, *The First Book of the Bible, Genesis* (New York: KTAV, 1974), 23–24.

Touching the tree is not, as Cassuto maintains, the same as eating its fruit, although touching the tree could lead to eating its fruit.

EARLY CHRISTIAN INTERPRETERS

AMBROSE OF MILAN

St. Ambrose (AD 337–397) took the view that the woman added to God's original command, and he thought the act of adding to it made her more susceptible to sin:

> There was nothing inexact about the command itself. The error lay in the report of the command. We realize that we ought not to make any addition to a command even by way of instruction. Any addition or qualification of a command is in the nature of a falsification. The simple, original form of a command should be preserved or the facts should be duly set before us. It frequently happens that a witness adds something of himself to a relation of facts. In this way, by the injection of an untruth, confidence in his testimony is wholly shattered. No addition therefore—not even a good one—is called for. What is, therefore, at first sight objectionable in the addition made by the woman: "Neither shall you touch anything of it"? God did not say this, but, rather: "you must not eat." Still, we have something here which leads to error.[11]

Ambrose recognizes that adding to what God said is no small matter: the woman made an "error" when she reported the command, and "we ought not to make any addition to a command even

---

11. Ambrose, *Hexameron, Paradise, and Cain and Abel*, trans. John J. Savage, The Fathers of the Church 42 (Washington, DC: The Catholic University of America Press, 1961), 335–36.

by way of instruction." If she added to God's command in order to provide further "instruction" or guidance (to herself?), or elucidation (to the serpent?), such an "addition or qualification of a command is in the nature of a falsification." When she added to what God said, "we have something here which leads to error." Ambrose recognizes that adding to what God said amounts to a falsification. Understandably it must be so, because it claims God said something he did not say. When Ambrose says the addition "leads to error," however, he has apparently not penetrated to the core of what he has already affirmed: falsification is already error. At exactly this point we encounter the kernel of the interpretive problem: if the woman added to what God said, she is already a falsifier and so already a sinner. She has erred or wandered from the truth. She has "missed the mark," to quote one definition of sin (חטאת, ἁμαρτία).

Ambrose now pursues another possibility: What if Adam was the one who added to what God had said? Then the picture would change:

> Many believe that this was Adam's fault—not the woman's. They reason that Adam in his desire to make her more cautious had said to the woman that God had given the additional instruction: "Neither shall you touch it." We know that it was not Eve, but Adam, who received the command from God, because the woman had not yet been created. Scripture does not reveal the exact words that Adam used when he disclosed to her the nature and content of the command. At all events, we understand that the substance of the command was given to the woman by the man. What opinions others have offered on this subject should be taken into consideration. It seems to me, however, that the initial violation and deceit was [sic] due to the woman.[12]

---

12. Ambrose, *Hexameron, Paradise, and Cain and Abel*, 336.

Ambrose does not explore the profound problem created if Adam
lied to his wife about God's command. He recognizes that if the
woman added to what God said, then "the initial violation and
deceit was due to the woman." But in that case, the woman was
a violator and deceiver even before she took the fruit. How can
Ambrose conclude it was the woman and not the man who was first
at fault? He does so by citing later biblical revelation:

> Although there may appear to be an element of uncertainty
> in deciding which of the two was guilty, we can discern the
> sex which was liable first to do wrong. Add to this the fact
> that she stands convicted in court whose previous error is
> afterward revealed. The woman is responsible for the man's
> error and not vice-versa. Hence Paul says: "Adam was not
> deceived, but the woman was deceived and was in sin."[13]

Ambrose appeals to later Scripture for his analysis of the woman's response. A biblical theologian would do the same: understand
the Old Testament with the help of the New Testament when possible. In this case the New Testament can shed light on the Old,
but perhaps not exactly in the way Ambrose has said. When Paul
says, "Adam was not the one deceived; it was the woman who was
deceived and became a sinner" (1 Tim 2:14), he tells us two things:
(1) Adam was not deceived, and therefore, when he sinned he did so
with his eyes wide open—but consequently, the woman was not, as
Ambrose says, "responsible for the man's error"; (2) the woman was
deceived and became a sinner (ἡ δὲ γυνὴ ἐξαπατηθεῖσα ἐν παραβάσει
γέγονεν, "but the woman, having been deceived, came into transgression"; 1 Tim 2:14). Paul does not tell us, as Ambrose could be
thought to imply, that the woman had herself become a deceiver

---

13. Ambrose, *Hexameron, Paradise, and Cain and Abel*, 336–37, with reference to
1 Tim 2:14.

(of her husband). He does tell us that, once she was deceived, she then sinned or "came into transgression." In other words, she was deceived (by the serpent), and then, in that state of being deceived, she became a transgressor by eating the forbidden fruit. Paul's analysis is in line with what the woman confessed to the Lord: "The serpent deceived me, and I ate" (Gen 3:13b).

CHRYSOSTOM

St. John Chrysostom (d. AD 407) took a much simpler view of the matter. He apparently assumed the Lord gave the same command the woman relayed to the serpent:

> She revealed the secret of the instruction and told him what God had said to them, and thus received from him a different kind of advice, bringing ruin and death. That is to say, when the woman said, "We do eat of every tree of the garden; but of the fruit of the tree in the middle of the garden God said, Do not eat or even touch it," that evil creature, enemy of our salvation, in his turn offered advice at odds with that of the Lord. You see, whereas the loving God had forbidden their tasting that fruit on account of his great care for them lest they be subject to death for their disobedience, that evil creature said to the woman "'*You will not truly die.*'" [Gen 3:4] What kind of excuse could anyone find appropriate to the woman for being prepared to give her complete attention to the creature that spoke with such temerity? I mean, after God said, "*Do not touch it lest you die,*" he said, "*You will not truly die.*" Then, not being satisfied with contradicting the words of God, he goes on to misrepresent the Creator as jealous so as to be in a position to introduce deceit by this means, get the better of the woman and carry out his own purpose. "*You will not truly die,*" he said. "*God, you see, knows*

that on the day that you eat of it, your eyes will be opened and
you will be like gods, knowing good and evil." [Gen 3:5] See all
the bait he offered: he filled the cup with a harmful drug
and gave it to the woman, who did not want to recognize its
deadly character. She could have known this from the outset,
had she wanted; instead, she listened to his word, that God
forbade their tasting the fruit for that reason *"He knows that*
your eyes will be opened and you will be like gods, knowing good
from evil" puffed up as she was with the hope of being equal
to God and evidently dreaming of greatness.[14]

Chrysostom's translation takes into account the ambiguity of the
key noun, "You will be like God/gods [Heb. אלהים]." Not all commentators mention this ambiguity. Beyond that, he verges on probing
the woman's psyche, as other commentators have done: "What kind
of excuse could anyone find appropriate to the woman for being
prepared to give her complete attention to the creature that spoke
with such temerity?" The question, nonetheless, is a good one. If the
woman was "prepared to give her complete attention" to a creature
that was so disrespectful toward God, that could imply other questions. How much did the woman know the Lord, or know of him,
at that point? Did she know so little of him that she could take the
serpent's characterization of God as possibly true? The questions
cannot be answered, of course, because no one under heaven can
know the answer. One could propose that the woman was, at this
point, on her way to being deceived, and once she was, she became
a sinner. His other analytical statement regarding her may not be
far from the truth: after she heard the serpent's second statement—
his false claim about God and the tree—she was (or better, became)
"puffed up … with the hope of being equal to God and evidently

---

14. St. Chrysostom, *Homilies on Genesis*, 312–13.

dreaming of greatness." But again, one cannot really know what she thought immediately after she heard the serpent's words. We are told that "when the woman saw that the tree was good for food, that it was pleasant to the eyes, and a tree desirable to make one wise, she took of its fruit and ate" (Gen 3:6 NKJV).

AUGUSTINE

St. Augustine, bishop of Hippo (AD 354–430), took a highly spiritualized view of the early chapters of Genesis, to the extent that he was not sure Eden was a literal place or the interaction between the woman and the serpent an actual conversation between a woman and a snake. He proposed that the serpent was not in Eden:

> For paradise signifies the happy life, as I said above, and the serpent was not present there, because he was already the devil and had fallen from his happiness because "he did not stand in the truth." We should not be surprised that he was able to speak with the woman although she was in paradise and he was not. For perhaps she was not in paradise according to place, but rather according to the disposition of happiness. Or, even if there is such a place which is called paradise in which Adam and Eve dwelled corporeally, do we have also to understand the devil's approach as corporeal? Of course not! [His approach was] rather spiritual, as the Apostle says, "According to the prince of the power of the air, of the spirit who now is at work in the children of disbelief."[15]

The accounts of Genesis 2 and 3 are very straightforward. The most natural reading of them is also straightforward: it would

---

15. Augustine, *On Genesis: Two Books on Genesis against the Manichees, and On the Literal Interpretation of Genesis: An Unfinished Book*, trans. Roland J. Teske, SJ, The Fathers of the Church 84 (Washington, DC: The Catholic University of America Press, 1991), 115–16. Augustine quotes John 8:44 and Eph 2:2.

appear there was a garden, there was a woman, there was a serpent, etc. Nonetheless, Augustine offers a highly spiritualized way of reading them. He notes the physical reality of the elements in the account only as a possibility that is not essential to what transpired: "even if there is such a place which is called paradise in which Adam and Eve dwelled corporeally." He infers that, because the devil is *now* at work as a spirit in people, and was in Paul's day, it must have been so with our first parents, wherever they were: he was a spirit, invisible, an influence.

Augustine next applies an allegory to human nature: "Still he deceives by means of the woman. Nor can our reason be brought to the consent that is sin, except when delight is aroused in that part of the soul which ought to obey reason as its ruling husband."[16] Because of this allegorical approach, it does not seem to matter whether or not the woman added to what God said. Augustine does seem to think the woman simply repeats God's original command: "For, when she was asked, the woman told him [i.e., the serpent] what they had been commanded."[17] The allegorical context, however, apparently makes the potential issue of any disagreement between Genesis 2:17b and Genesis 3:3b unimportant as a matter of historiography. For Augustine the woman in the account has become an allegorical figure who represents the soul's appetitive side, and her husband becomes an allegorical figure who represents reason:

> Even now nothing else happens in each of us when one falls into sin than occurred then in those three: the serpent, the woman and the man. For first the suggestion is made, whether by thought or by the senses of the body, by seeing or touching or hearing or tasting or smelling. When this suggestion has been made, if our desire is not aroused toward

16. Augustine, *On Genesis*, 117.
17. Augustine, *On Genesis*, 118.

sinning, the cunning of the serpent will be excluded. If, however, it is aroused, it will be as though the woman were already persuaded. At times reason checks and suppresses in a virile way even desire that has been aroused. When this happens, we do not fall into sin, but we are crowned for our modest struggle. But if reason consents and decides that what desire has stirred up should be carried out, man is expelled from the whole happy life as if from paradise.[18]

In a traditional view of the relation of husband to wife, in which the husband is head of the wife as Christ is head of the church, Augustine's ingenious analysis may have value for some as a portrayal of spiritual dynamics. It is not, however—nor does it aim or claim to be—an exegesis of literal historical events. For Augustine the temptation account of Genesis 3:1–6 is an allegory that can be instructive for readers after the fall.

SUMMARY COMMENTS

A brief survey of Jewish and early Christian commentators on the woman's reply to the serpent has shown a few points that recur in Reformation and post-Reformation interpretation as well as some that do not. The results of the survey may be summarized as follows.

1. Some commentators thought Adam was not completely truthful to his wife regarding the tree. This view seems to consider the woman to be "the weaker vessel," to borrow Peter's term (1 Pet 3:7 NKJV):

    a) Adam added to what God had said, as a further safeguard lest his wife touch the tree (e.g., R. Nathan).

---

18. Augustine, *On Genesis*, 117.

The reasoning is that if she touched it she might be more inclined to go beyond mere touch and eat it.

b) Adam omitted its designation as the tree of the knowledge of good and evil, lest "if he told her she would crave to eat of it" (R. Meir Zlotowitz).

2. Most commentators have thought the woman added to what God had said. The views however are somewhat varied:

a) She did so as a precautionary measure of her own invention (Philo).

b) She unwittingly diminished it by adding to it (Babylonian Talmud, Rashi).

c) She added the words "nor shall you touch it," but this was tantamount to saying, "You shall not eat of it" (Cassuto).

d) She added to it and by doing so made herself more susceptible to sin (Ambrose).

3. A minority view has held that the woman did not add to what God said but simply reported what God had said:

a) Chrysostom presents this view in a very straightforward way and without argumentation to support it.

b) Augustine does the same, although for him the allegorical meaning is of paramount importance, and thus it does not seem to matter whether or not the woman added to what God said.

c) Benno Jacob also presents this view, but with little argument to support it.

Another thing to note about the early interpreters is that they may be cautionary examples of how far speculation can go. Modern commentators are not likely to come up with ideas such as, "When the snake saw that she was lying to him, he took her and pushed her against the tree" (R. Hiyya), or "This world lost out on a great benefit, for if things had not happened the way they did, a man could send commerce through [a snake], who would come and go [doing his employer's business]" (R. Simeon b. Eleazar), or "What did the wicked serpent then do? He touched the tree with his hands and feet and shook it so hard that some of its fruit fell to the ground. ... Then he said to her '[You see? So likewise] you say that God has forbidden us to eat from the tree. But I can eat from it and not die, and so can you'" (R. Nathan). Modern commentators also are not likely to spiritualize the passage as Augustine did, so that the serpent represents allure, the woman our appetitive nature, and Adam the controlling husband, reason, who is able keep our appetite in check. Commentators from the Reformation onward have, as we will see, engaged in ways of interpretation that could be just as difficult to substantiate, although they are less fanciful. The following chapter will consider some of them.

3

HISTORY OF INTERPRETATION: REFORMATION ONWARD

A review of Jewish and early Christian interpreters of the woman's response to the serpent indicates they held, for the most part, one of two views: (1) Adam told his wife the wrong thing (adding the words, "and you shall not touch it"), which she then repeated to the serpent, or (2) the woman herself added those words that the Lord had not said. Interpreters from Luther onward have held one or the other of these views almost without exception, whether or not they have been in the mainstream of evangelical tradition regarding Mosaic authorship of the Pentateuch. This study will consider Luther and Calvin first, then the views of critical scholars, and finally the views of evangelical scholars from the late nineteenth century to the present day. The resulting overview consequently will be largely chronological.

EARLY REFORMATION VIEWS

MARTIN LUTHER

Luther believes the woman added something of her own to what the Lord said in Genesis 2, but he does not fault her for adding the

words, "neither shall you touch it." For Luther, her unwarranted
addition was the term "lest" ("lest perchance" is Luther's paraphrase):

> Eve's beginnings are successful enough. She makes a dis-
> tinction between all the other trees of the garden and this
> tree. She rehearses the commandment of God. But when she
> comes to relate also the punishment, she fails. She does not
> relate the punishment, as it had been declared by the Lord.
> The Lord had said, absolutely, "For in the day that thou
> eatest thereof, thou shalt surely die," Gen 2:17. Out of this
> absolute declaration, Eve makes an expression, not absolute,
> "Lest perchance ye should die."[1]

This viewpoint will be discussed later in connection with Calvin's
very similar evaluation of the woman's response. But if Luther is
right, the woman's alteration of what the Lord had said would be an
act of faithlessness, on the understanding that faith is amening the
Lord's Being and doing. Luther does not explore the idea of biblical
faith as amening God, but he does see her supposed misstatement
as an act of unbelief:

> This defect in the statement of Eve is very remarkable, and
> demands particular observation; for it proves that she had
> turned aside from faith to unbelief. For as the promise of
> God demands faith, so the threatening of God demands
> faith also. Eve ought to have made her statement as a fact,
> and a certainty. "If I eat, I shall surely die." This faith how-
> ever Satan so assails, with his insidious speech, as to induce
> Eve to add the expression, "perchance." For the devil had
> effectually persuaded her to think that God surely was not

---

1. Martin Luther, *A Critical and Devotional Commentary on Genesis*, trans. John
Nicholas Lenker (Minneapolis: Lutherans in All Lands Co., 1904).

so cruel as to kill her for merely tasting a fruit. Hence the heart of Eve was now filled with the poison of Satan.[2]

Luther's whole argument depends on the translation of one Hebrew word, פֶּן (*pen*), translated "*lest* ye die" (KJV), or by Luther, "Lest perchance ye should die" (but cf. "*daß* ihr nicht sterbt," "*that* you die not" in his 1545 translation of the Bible). Although Luther translated in a fairly forceful way, he argues for a weaker meaning:

This text therefore is also by no means properly translated in our version. The meaning of the original Hebrew is that Eve speaks her own words; whereas she is ostensibly reciting the Word of God; and that she adds to the Word of God her own expression, "perchance." Wherefore the artifice of the lying spirit has completely succeeded. For the object which he especially had in view; namely, to draw Eve away from the Word and from faith; he has now so far accomplished, as to cause Eve to corrupt the Word of God; or, to use the expression of Paul, "he has turned her aside from the will of God, and caused her to go after Satan," 1 Tim. 5:15. And the beginning of certain ruin is to be turned aside from God, and to be turned after Satan; that is, not to stand firmly in the Word and in faith. When Satan therefore sees this beginning in Eve, he plies against her his whole power as against a bowing wall, until she falls prostrate on the ground.[3]

Whether or not Luther had Paul's definition of faith in mind, his statement agrees with what Paul wrote: "Whatever is not of faith is sin" (Rom 4:23 NKJV). Accordingly the woman is already in sin when she modifies God's word—if what she did was a real modification in

---

2. Luther, *Commentary on Genesis*.

3. Luther, *Commentary on Genesis*.

meaning, as Luther has it, and not just a paraphrase. And yet there is a potential problem with this understanding, for Paul also says, "It was the woman who was deceived and became a sinner" (ἡ δὲ γυνὴ ἐξαπατηθεῖσα ἐν παραβάσει γέγονεν, 1 Tim 2:14 NIV; compare, "But the woman being deceived was in the transgression," KJV). Is it true that "the devil had effectually persuaded her to think that God surely was not so cruel as to kill her for merely tasting a fruit"? There is no way to prove this. But if Luther is right, she was already deceived.

Luther's argument is perhaps the most potent of the ones so far encountered or to be encountered. Its force lies in the idea that if the woman weakened God's word she was saying untruth; that is an act of unbelief and, consequently, is sin. Paul, however, makes it clear that deception is what produced a sinful state in her. The question is whether one can insist that she was in a state of deception when she first responded to the serpent, and herein lies both the power of and the problem with Luther's view. If one is to agree with Luther, one must affirm that the woman is instantly deceived by the serpent's question so that she answers in unbelief. One might think this view—quite apart from the fact that it rests on a questionable translation of the Hebrew (see below)—strains credibility. The unfolding of the narrative seems to argue against it because the serpent takes additional time to develop an argument regarding the fruit (Gen 3:4–5). The argument finally proves successful since it causes the woman to look at the fruit, see its goodness, and finally transgress and take the fruit. The sequence is the first case of falling into sin that uses those words, "see" (ראה), "good" (טוב), and "take" (לקח), as many have noted.[4] Apparently once one has embraced deception, one is in sin because one is amening a view of things

---

4. The same sequence occurs with the "sons of God" (Gen 6:2) and with Achan (Josh 7:21); apparently it is used to denote what John calls "the lust of the eyes," leading to a sinful taking; cf. Niehaus, *BT* 1, 100, 190.

that is not true (compare the warning in Heb 4:13). But it seems impossible to prove that the woman was already deceived when she answered the serpent's question; moreover it seems unlikely she was deceived at that moment, since the serpent had not yet said anything to deceive her.

JOHN CALVIN

John Calvin appears to follow Luther's reasoning, both regarding the woman's supposed addition ("you shall not touch") and the modification involved with her use of the Hebrew, פֶּן (pen), which Luther translated "lest perchance":

> When she says, God has forbidden them to eat or to touch, some suppose the second word to be added for the purpose of charging God with too great severity, because he prohibited them even from the touch. But I rather understand that she hitherto remained in obedience, and expressed her pious disposition by anxiously observing the precept of God; only, in proclaiming the punishment, she begins to give ways by inserting the adverb "perhaps," when God has certainly pronounced, "Ye shall die the death." For although with the Hebrews פֶּן (pen) does not always imply doubt, yet, since it is generally taken in this sense, I willingly embrace the opinion that the woman was beginning to waver. Certainly, she had not death so immediately before her eyes, should she become disobedient to God, as she ought to have had. She clearly proves that her perception of the true danger of death was distant and cold.[5]

---

5. John Calvin, *Commentaries on the First Book of Moses Called Genesis, Volume First*, trans. Rev. John King (Grand Rapids: Eerdmans, 1948), 149.

A great deal in this view depends on one's translation of the adverb פֶּן. The Hebrew adverb does not necessarily imply doubt. One reads in Psalm 2:12, "Kiss the Son, lest [פֶּן] He be angry, / And you perish in the way" (NKJV)—a consequence of which there should be no room for doubt. John Gill later noted they would have to touch it to eat it, so touching was implied in Genesis 2:17 (an understanding close to what Cassuto later espoused). Regarding the adverb in Genesis 3:3, Gill noted: "As if it was a matter of doubt, when it was most strongly assured; for the word [sc. פֶּן] is not always to be understood of doubting, but of the event of a thing; see Ps 2:12; and may be rendered, that ye die not; which would certainly be the case, should they pluck the fruit and eat of it."[6]

CRITICAL SCHOLARLY TRADITION

Critical scholars seem not to have been concerned with the translation of פֶּן. They have, however, taken the time-honored view that the woman added to what God told Adam. Their affirmation of an older perspective in this one matter does not mean they affirm or assume the historicity of the text. We turn now to some examples of critical scholarship.

S. R. DRIVER

One of the best-known and most influential higher-critical scholars in the English-speaking world, S. R. Driver, draws on Peter's language about women for his interpretation of the woman's conduct, and remarks:

> The serpent begins by addressing the woman, the weaker
> vessel, who moreover had not herself actually heard the pro-
> hibition (ii. 16 f.). It first distorts the prohibition, and then

---

6. John Gill, *An Exposition of the First Book of Moses Called Genesis* (1778, 1810; repr., Springfield: Particular Baptist Press, 2010), 53.

affects surprise at it when thus distorted; thus it artfully sows doubts and suspicions in the heart of the unsuspecting woman, and at the same time insinuates that it is itself qualified to judge of the propriety of such a prohibition. ... The woman corrects the serpent; and to show how fully aware she is of the strictness of the prohibition, adds (what is not contained in ii. 16 f.) that they are not even to touch the fruit of the tree.[7]

Driver explains the woman's state of mind when she heard and then answered the serpent's question: he says the serpent "sows doubts and suspicions" in the woman's heart. That is a reasonable inference, and it may be true, but there is no way to verify whether it is true or not. The serpent seems to attempt to sow doubts and suspicions, but we are not told that he succeeds in doing so at this point in the narrative.[8] Driver ascribes a motive for her addition of the prohibition of touch "to show how fully aware she is of the strictness of the prohibition." This, too, could seem to be a reasonable inference, but the text does not mention this motivation, which Driver attributes to the woman.

HERMANN GUNKEL

Gunkel, similarly, imputes a misplaced zeal to the woman. He is fully in the camp of those who want to see both detail and depth

---

7. S. R. Driver, *The Book of Genesis with Introduction and Notes* (London: Methuen & Co. Ltd., 1904), 44–45. Cf. earlier in the tradition of critical scholarship: A. Dillmann, *Genesis Critically and Exegetically Expounded,* vol. 1, trans. Wm. B. Stevenson (Edinburgh: T&T Clark, 1897), 150–51; Thomas J. Conant, *The Book of Genesis* (New York: American Bible Union, 1868), 15.

8. See, similarly, Marcus Dods, *Genesis* (Edinburgh: T&T Clark, 1905), 15, regarding the same moment in the narrative: "He [sc. the serpent] insinuates into the woman's mind distrust of God."

of psychological portrayal in the encounter between the serpent
and the woman:

> The subsequent narrative has always excited the delight
> of sensitive readers through its mastery of psychological
> description. In the few words and actions with which he
> describes his characters, the narrator makes their inner lives
> clear. His masterpiece is the description of the woman. The
> serpent, bitterly evil and sly, wants to harm God and seduce
> the people. It turns to the woman. Why to the Woman? The
> woman is livelier, more appetitive, and awakens earlier than
> the man. A highly interesting, even piquant scene follows. In
> childish, trusting harmlessness, the young, inexperienced
> woman stands before it. She does not suspect how ruinous
> the words of the evil serpent are. The symbols of childishly
> dull innocence and of sly seduction stand alongside one
> another. "Did God really say?" The serpent possesses won-
> drous knowledge. It has heard—the narrator does not betray
> how—of God's prohibition to the people. Now it takes the
> position that it has only imprecise information and would
> like now to be precisely informed by the people themselves.
> It greatly exaggerates God's prohibition and acts as though
> it were astonished at such harshness. ... Thus, it ingrati-
> ates itself through pretended sympathy and sows mistrust
> and suspicion toward God in the heart of the unsuspect-
> ing wife. ... She is quick, however, to reject the ignomini-
> ous suspicion and zealously emphasizes the permission. ...
> The element is meant to portray the zealous nature of the
> young woman.[9]

9. Hermann Gunkel, *Genesis Translated and Interpreted*, trans. Mark E. Biddle
(Macon, GA: Mercer University Press, 1997), 16.

Anyone who has read Gunkel can attest that he is not lacking in literary sensitivity. His work on the Psalms, while not without theological difficulties, is a remarkable accomplishment in the world of literary form criticism. However, what he has written about the "mastery of psychological description" in the Genesis 3 account is a mix of suggestions that would appear plausible (especially regarding the intentions of the serpent, since it soon becomes clear that he is quite against God and God's purposes), and statements for which there would appear to be no explicit evidence in the text. To itemize:

1. Gunkel states, "Why to the Woman? The woman is livelier, more appetitive, and awakens earlier than the man." How can one know she is "livelier, more appetitive, and awakens earlier than the man"?

2. Another question, possibly less important, is raised by the statement, "[The serpent] would like now to be precisely informed by *the people themselves*" (emphasis added). One would like to see this statement developed further—for example, what is meant by "the people themselves." The subsequent narrative gives the impression that the woman was alone when the serpent spoke to her, and this has been the usual understanding in the history of interpretation. The serpent is presented as speaking to the woman and to no one else. As has been indicated, the plural verb forms can be accounted for on that understanding.[10] At best, the point is ambiguous.

---

10. On the translation of Gen 3:6b, a statement that is itself ambiguous, cf. Niehaus, *BT* 1, 100–102. The verse does not make a case that (contrary somehow to the impression created by Gen 3:2–3; cf. 1 Tim 2:14) Adam was standing by but did nothing while the woman and the serpent conversed.

3. Gunkel also affirms, "She is quick, however, to reject
    the ignominious suspicion and zealously emphasizes
    the permission." How can one know she reacts to the
    question as ignominious, rather than just erroneous?
    How does one know she is not simply answering the
    serpent's question? How can one know she is empha-
    sizing the permission rather than just repeating it?
    How can one know she is responding "zealously"?

Gunkel is certainly right to invite his readers to consider the
psychological implications of the narrative in Genesis 3:1–3. The
problem in attempting to do so, however, lies in the laconic nature
of the material. Certain inferences may be true, but they remain
inferences unless some later passage in the Bible sheds further light
on them. In this case, what Paul says about the progress of deception
and sin in the woman is as much as one finds, and Paul's statement is
laconic enough. One might wish for a more nuanced analysis of the
woman's response to the serpent, but it does not appear that either
her reported speech or later biblical commentary offers enough to
support unambiguously any deeper analysis.

Gunkel shares with Bonhoeffer and Barth an assumption that
the material is not history but, rather, imaginative literature. That
view was common in the critical environment of German biblical
scholarship in his day. As noted with Barth and Bonhoeffer, the
assumption may give him a sense of freedom to interpret the text
imaginatively. In another regard Gunkel, perhaps not surprisingly,
imputes to the woman the sort of motives we, too, could have. But
such motives would be sin (not amening God), before she took the
fruit, and the woman is nowhere in the Bible accused of having
them. Perhaps as importantly, the passage in question does not
make it clear that she has them.

GERHARD VON RAD

Driver tells us the woman added to what God said "to show how fully aware she is of the strictness of the provision." Gunkel somewhat differently says she "zealously emphasizes the permission." Such nuanced interpretations, while possible and plausible (although somewhat at odds with each other), cannot be established unambiguously from the limited facts of the laconic narrative segment of Genesis 3:1–3. Gerhard von Rad, in the same critical tradition, follows in a similar vein:

> In the form of this question, however, the serpent has already made a deadly attack on the artlessness of obedience. ... The woman is quite ingenuous with regard to this malice. She corrects the distortion but in doing so goes a bit too far in her zeal. God did withhold only *one* tree from man (this part of the narrative does not seem to know of the tree of life), but God did not say it should not even be touched. This additional word already shows a slight weakness in the woman's position. It is as though she wanted to set a law for herself by means of this exaggeration.[11]

Here again the interpretation offers intriguing possibilities, for which, unfortunately, there is no substantiation in the text:

1. How do we know the woman has a "zeal" as a result of which she goes a bit too far? The verses (Gen 3:2–3) do not, apparently, say anything about the woman's zeal, and nothing in the Bible says she went too far in her reply to the serpent at this point in the narrative.

---

11. Gerhard von Rad, *Genesis: A Commentary* (Philadelphia: Westminster John Knox Press, 1973), 88.

2. How can one know "it is as though she wanted to set
    a law for herself"? This may be plausible—humans
    today do it often enough—but again, the text does not
    say so.

3. How can one be sure that what the woman says is
    an "exaggeration"? No other possibility is mentioned,
    although the history of interpretation has offered sev-
    eral alternatives, including (though rarely) the one
    advocated in the present work.

Plausible and even attractive as these possibilities may be, the
account reports none of them. Von Rad also comments, "This part
of the narrative does not seem to know of the tree of life," but the
apparent contradiction disappears if one reads Genesis 2–3 as a
continuous narrative.[12]

The question does invite review of another matter that has
already received some consideration: What about the tree of life?
The Lord has not forbidden eating from that tree. He does act to prevent it after the fall. But there is no way to know whether Adam and
his wife were able to eat or had eaten from that tree before the fall.
Perhaps eating of it only once would confer immortal life, but that
is not what the Lord says. The Lord says, "The man has now become
like one of us, knowing good and evil. He must not be allowed to
reach out his hand and take also from the tree of life and eat, and
live forever" (Gen 3:22). It could be that *regularly* eating from the tree
of life would keep one alive forever. On the other hand, the Hebrew
word [עוֹלָם] translated "forever" does not necessarily mean "forever."
The root idea is apparently to be "hidden" from view. With regard
to time, then, it means something is so far in the past or so far in

---

12. And not as a practitioner of, e.g., source criticism or kindred hermeneutical
methods.

the future that it is out of sight. So Isaiah refers to "the days of old [עולם], / the days of Moses and his people" (Isa 63:11). From Isaiah's point in time, the days of Moses were temporally remote—hidden from view.[13] Maybe Adam and his wife could have eaten the fruit of that tree at any time before the fall. Maybe doing so repeatedly would have sustained their life in some special way. That seems to be its property in any view of how often one might eat of it. After the Lord put Adam in the garden with the tree of life (Gen 2:9) he said, "You are free to eat from *any/every* [כל] tree in the garden" (Gen 2:16, emphasis added). "Any/every tree" would include the tree of life.[14] The Lord God gave no command against eating the fruit of that tree.[15] Perhaps Adam and his wife would have continued to have life—sustained by the Lord from day to day—without eating the fruit of the tree of life but would have been allowed to eat that fruit once, or regularly, and *then* live forever, after they had successfully withstood the temptations of the serpent, who had not yet appeared. But the text does not report these things, however much one might wish that it did. One may hold these ideas as intriguing but unverified. The Lord may have instructed Adam about any of them, but the laconic narrative does not tell us so.

---

13. Cf. definitions and examples of this somewhat mysterious term in: *BDB*, 761; William L. Holladay, ed., *A Concise Hebrew and Aramaic Lexicon of the Old Testament* (Grand Rapids: Eerdmans, 1971), 267–68; *HALOT*, II, 798–99, 834–35; *DCH*, VI, 300–7, 427–28. Cf. extensive discussion of the root by Ernst Jenni, "Das Wort ōlām im Alten Testament," *ZAW*, Band 64, 1952 (Berlin: Töpelmann, 1953), 197–248; continued in *ZAW* 65, 1953 (Berlin: Töpelmann, 1953), 1–35. Jenni notes the derivation of עולם from the verb "to hide" (ע ל ם) affirmed separately by König, Gesenius, and Orelli, but Jenni concludes that one cannot be sure of the root from which the word is derived.

14. Cf. discussion in *BT* 2, 14–15.

15. One might assume they had not yet eaten of it and thus had not yet become immortal before the fall, but that is just an assumption—assuming that eating its fruit only once conferred eternal physical life.

CLAUS WESTERMANN

Westermann, the last critical scholar to be considered here, builds on the tradition of Gunkel and von Rad. He characterizes the woman's response to the serpent as follows:

> The woman counters the serpent by stating correctly the command of God. The command is not harsh; they can eat from all the trees in the garden, with one exception, so that they do not die. They are provided for and at the same time protected from danger. But while the command of God is being discussed, it is altered in the very act of defending it. The narrator makes this known by means of the slight refinement that the woman introduced: "Neither shall you touch it." God had not said that. G. von Rad explains: "It is as though she wanted to set a law for herself by means of this exaggeration." This sentence makes it clear that a command that is questioned is no longer the original command, as the continuation of the narrative makes even clearer. One who defends a command can already be on the way to breaking it. V. 3 describes the forbidden tree only as "the tree in the middle of the garden." The sentence shows that the tree cannot yet be described as "the tree of the knowledge of good and evil" (so H. Gunkel).[16]

Westermann adopts ideas put forward by Gunkel and von Rad and takes the long-standing majority view regarding the relationship between Genesis 3:3b and Genesis 2:17b. The following points are worth noting:

---

16. Claus Westermann, *Genesis 1–11: A Continental Commentary*, trans. John J. Scullion, SJ (Minneapolis: Fortress, 1994), 329–30.

1. It is obvious the woman added to what God said in Genesis 2 ("God had not said that"). If one follows the evidence strictly, however, one cannot really say, "God had not said that." All one can say is, "God was not reported by anyone (before Gen 3:3b) as having said that."

2. Westermann observes that "a command that is questioned is no longer the original command." It may not be perfectly clear what Westermann means by this, and he does not explain it further, except to say, "the continuation of the narrative makes [this point] even clearer." What should be clear, however, is that at this point he is commenting on von Rad's statement ("It is as though she wanted to set a law for herself by means of this exaggeration") and not on what is actually reported in Genesis 3:3. In legal terms, it would seem the Lord's command is what it is. It may feel different, at different times, to the person who should obey it, but even if the person questions the command—or implicitly questions it, and then adds to it and so tries to make it stronger—the person's question does not change the command. Indeed, nothing the person can do would change God's command. Or perhaps he means that the woman questions the command, implicitly, by adding to it and thereby deprives the original command of its force in her own mind. She has not changed the command, but she has changed the way she views the command. There does not, however, appear to be anything in the material that says the woman questioned the Lord's command at this

point. The narrative (in Gen 3:2–3) reports only that she answered the serpent's question.

3. It certainly may be true that "one who defends a command can already be on the way to breaking it," but although breaking a command was in the woman's future, how can one know she was "on her way to breaking it" (presumably in her thoughts or feelings) at this point? The narrator has not yet told us about her thoughts. One cannot know that "it is as though she wanted to set a law for herself by means of this exaggeration," because there is no way to know it is an exaggeration. The first comment on her thoughts comes subsequently, when, after her talk with the serpent and after hearing his last words (vv. 4–5), she looks at the tree and begins to consider its attractions (v. 6). To suggest a more commonplace analogy: I may be obeying the speed limit when I notice the limit posted on the roadside and am still going at or below the posted limit—and I may even reason with myself on the importance of holding to the limit—but then subsequently accelerate, for whatever reason, and exceed the limit. At the initial moment, however, when I still observe the speed limit, and remind myself how important it is to obey the speed limit, or even think it would be safer to go slower than the limit (i.e., when I am in effect "defending the command"—to myself), I am not yet "on my way to breaking" the speed limit in my motives unless some inclination or intention to break it has already entered my mind. It may be that adding to God's command would diminish it in the woman's mind (making it seem weaker than it really

was because it had required her addition, "and you shall not touch it," to fortify it) and thereby make it feel easier to break—or, that my going slower than the limit (and thus "exaggerating" the severity of the posted limit to myself) might provoke a counterreaction and lead me to want to exceed the limit. These are possibilities. But there appears to be no evidence that any inclination or intention to break God's command had entered the woman's mind at this point in the narrative. Unfortunately, the observation about being on the way to breaking the command cannot tell us anything that can be documented about the woman's thoughts or motivations, because the text does not tell us what she had in mind at this point in her interaction with the serpent.

EVANGELICAL SCHOLARLY TRADITION

The critical tradition employs hermeneutics relatively unknown before it and also not normally employed by evangelical interpreters. Nonetheless, when it comes to understanding the material at hand, critical scholars build on a very old precritical tradition. Modern evangelical scholars have seen the contrast between Genesis 2 and 3 in the same way. So it would not be right to suggest that some evangelicals have followed their more liberal colleagues in this line of thought.[17]

---

17. As some evangelical scholars have, one way or another, followed the example of liberal scholars when they see more than one Abrahamic covenant in the materials of Genesis 15 and 17. For documentation and discussion, see Jeffrey J. Niehaus, "God's Covenant with Abraham," *JETS* 56.2 (2013): 249–71, and *BT* 2, chapter 4.

KEIL AND DELITZSCH

C. F. Keil and F. Delitzsch, late in the nineteenth century, explained the woman's response to the serpent's opening question as follows:

> Instead of turning away, the woman replied, "We may eat of the fruit of the trees of the garden; but of the fruit of the tree which is in the midst of the garden, God hath said, Ye shall not eat of it, neither shall ye touch it, lest ye die." She was aware of the prohibition, therefore, and fully understood its meaning; but she added, "neither shall ye touch it," and proved by this very exaggeration that it appeared too stringent even to her, and therefore that her love and confidence towards God were already beginning to waver. Here was the beginning of her fall: "for doubt is the father of sin, and skepsis the mother of all transgression; and in this father and this mother, all our present knowledge has a common origin with sin" (Ziegler).[18]

Whereas Westermann suggests the woman thought the command was weak and needed her addition, Keil and Delitzsch suggest she thought it was "too stringent." There are unfortunately two difficulties with this evaluation of the woman's response, and they appear in the comments of earlier interpreters and subsequent evangelical scholars: (1) Interpreters have tried to understand the woman's inner thought process and/or attitude on the basis of the data provided by verse 3, which are too limited to substantiate the conclusions reached or the interpretations suggested;[19] (2) In terms

---

18. C. F. Keil and F. Delitzsch, *Biblical Commentary on the Old Testament, Vol. 1: The Pentateuch* (Grand Rapids: Eerdmans, 1973), 94–95.

19. Cf. Herbert E. Ryle, *The Book of Genesis, The Cambridge Bible for Schools and Colleges,* ed. A. F. Kirkpatrick (Cambridge: University Press, 1914), 48, who sensibly observes regarding the account of the fall and Gen 3:1 in particular, "Vivid and

of methodology, no comparison has been made of the relationship between Genesis 2:17 and 3:2–3 and any other examples of third person or narratively "omniscient" reporting (as in Gen 2:17) vis-à-vis first person recounting of the same event (as in Gen 3:2–3). Such research could demonstrate the laconic aspect of reporting in those other cases and provide a comparative literary context for evaluating Genesis 3:2–3 vis-à-vis Genesis 2:17. It would appear that a comparison of the statements in Genesis 2 and 3 invites—one could even say, for the sake of thoroughness, *requires*—such an approach. It is hoped the present work will contribute to remedy this inexplicable lacuna in historiographical study of the two passages.

GEERHARDUS VOS

Our sampling of the history of interpretation continues with the comments of a well-known biblical theologian, Geerhardus Vos. Vos takes a similar view to that of his predecessors:

> And yet in the more or less indignant form of this denial there already shines through that the woman had begun to entertain the possibility of God's restricting her too severely. And by entertaining this, even for a moment, she had already begun to separate in principle between the rights of God and her own rights. In doing so she had admitted the seed of the act of sinning into her heart. And still further, in this direction goes the inexact form of her quoting the words of God: "ye shall not eat of it, neither shall ye touch it." In this unwarranted introduction of the denial of the privilege of

---

picturesque as it is, the story leaves many things omitted and unexplained. The present verse is an illustration."

"touching" the woman betrays a feeling, as though after all
God's measures may have been too harsh.[20]

Like commentators before him, Vos adds color and detail to the
laconic account presented in Genesis 3:2–3. The narrative however
reports only the woman's words, not her tone of voice or her feelings,
in verses 2–3. It is certainly possible that her reply to the serpent
was a "more or less indignant form of ... denial" or that "the woman
had begun to entertain the possibility of God's restricting her too
severely," but the text unfortunately does not report these thoughts
or feelings. There is no way to know that "the woman betrays a
feeling" when she adds (*if* she adds!) the restriction about touching,
"as though after all God's measures may have been too harsh." It is
understandable and natural to supply (or to want to supply) information about the woman's feelings or thought processes when she
answers the serpent. In courtroom settings, a defending or prose-
cuting attorney easily uses just that approach—imputing motives
on the basis of reported words or actions. Unfortunately, Genesis
3:2–3 report nothing more than the woman's words.

MEREDITH G. KLINE

Meredith Kline, as noted in chapter 1, follows this tradition. He
credits the woman with correcting the *serpent's* misrepresentation
of what God said but then in turn faults *her* for misrepresenting
what God said:

> She corrected Satan's expansion of the prohibition by stating
> that it did not extend to all the trees, but then she apparently
> expanded on the divine proscription herself by adding the
> restriction about touching the tree. If so, she was probably
> venting a feeling of resentment that the special prohibition

---

20. Geerhardus Vos, *Biblical Theology* (Grand Rapids: Eerdmans, 1975), 35.

was arbitrary and unfair, a critical feeling which betrayed an assumption that she had rights the Creator had not sufficiently respected.[21]

Kline's analysis helpfully allows the possibility of some ambiguity with the words "if so." Nonetheless, for him the likelihood falls against the woman: "She was probably venting a feeling of resentment." Her defense attorney might respond: she was probably *not* venting a feeling of resentment but merely conveying what she knew. Such an attorney might also question where the idea of the woman's rights comes from in this primordial case. It is not stated in the text, unless one considers God's permission to eat of any other tree a right. That may be the root of Kline's idea that being forbidden one tree felt like an unjust limitation of her rights (i.e., why not be permitted all trees?) But these ideas and motives are not reported in the text. People who have grown up in democratic countries, having the benefit of many rights, naturally may be highly aware of human-rights issues. One may speculate that, with such a background, Vos and Kline, American scholars, perhaps naturally assume a concern for rights on the part of the woman. But the text, unfortunately, speaks of no such motive. It might be a stretch to imagine that a human in an unfallen condition would be thinking of his or her own rights rather than being filled with wonder at their environment and gratitude toward their Creator.

ALLEN P. ROSS

Allen P. Ross has presented a more detailed discussion of the woman's encounter with the serpent than any other scholar mentioned so far. He has analyzed the differences between the woman's version

---

21. Meredith G. Kline, *Kingdom Prologue: Genesis Foundations for a Covenantal Worldview* (Overland Park, KS: Two Age Press, 2000), 124.

of God's command in Genesis 3 and the reported command itself in Genesis 2. His argument stands in the majority tradition of interpretation:

> In the woman's response to the serpent's question, it becomes clear that the precision of the Word of the Lord had not been retained. There are three changes that she made. First, she minimized the provision of the Lord. The Lord had said, "You may freely eat" ... but Eve simply said, "We may eat." ... Second, she added to the prohibition. The Lord had said nothing about touching the tree, but Eve said that God [she used the serpent's designation] said, "Neither shall you touch it." ... Von Rad says that it is as though she wanted to set a law for herself by means of this exaggeration [*Genesis*, p. 86]. Third, she weakened the penalty for the sin. God had declared, "You shall surely die" ... but Eve said, "lest you die." ... Concentration on such a forbidden object very easily led her to these modifications—unless Adam had told her incorrectly.[22]

A reader not predisposed to sympathy with these characterizations might think they appear prejudicial or maybe even prosecutorial. Ross acknowledges that the changes made "are within the legitimate range of interpretation" (see below), but he unfortunately appears to introduce all of them negatively. Each statement requires examination in its own right in order that the full force of this approach may be seen.

---

22. Allen P. Ross, *Creation and Blessing: A Guide to the Study and Exposition of the Book of Genesis* (Grand Rapids: Baker Academic, 1988), 134–35. The quote is complete, although not including Hebrew transliterations.

1. First, "it becomes clear that the precision of the Word
    of the Lord had not been retained." As Ross allows, a
    statement made in indirect discourse is "within the
    legitimate range of interpretation." On the other hand,
    to say "the precision of the Word of the Lord had not
    been retained" presents a different conclusion. It char-
    acterizes the woman's statements as flawed. As has
    been noted, if such were the case, the woman would
    already be in sin, not fully amening the Lord—fail-
    ing to retain the precision of God's word when she
    should have retained it. On such a view—without
    qualification—any paraphrase would appear to be
    sin by definition. The only sinless response possible
    for the woman would have been to repeat the Lord's
    ipsissima verba.

2. Second, "she minimized the provision of the Lord." If
    she minimized it, rather than just paraphrasing it in
    the natural flow of conversation, does that perhaps
    imply she had some motive for reducing its force?[23]

3. Third, "she added to the prohibition." As we have seen,
    this would be a sin, whether the addition is deliber-
    ate or not. In this regard, Ross quotes as supporting
    material von Rad's comment (discussed above), "It is
    as though she wanted to set a law for herself by means
    of this exaggeration." But that, too, would be more spe-
    cifically sin: setting herself up as lawgiver in the Lord's
    place. Nonetheless, it has not been demonstrated that
    she exaggerated what God said.

---

23. G. K. Beale, who follows Ross's analysis, elaborates on this possibility (see
below).

4. The next comment is, "she weakened the penalty for the sin." This would appear to be a negative evaluation of a summary made in indirect discourse.

5. Finally, Ross raises the possibility that Adam had misinformed his wife: "Concentration on such a forbidden object very easily led her to these modifications—unless Adam had told her incorrectly." As has been understood, however, had Adam told her incorrectly he would already have been in sin, on the same understanding of what sin is (cf. Rom 14:23b). Adam himself would have been misrepresenting the Lord's words—attributing to the Lord words the Lord had not spoken. One should also note there is no evidence that, at this point, the woman had begun to "[concentrate] on such a forbidden object." She seems to concentrate on it only later—"When the woman saw that the fruit of the tree was good for food and pleasing to the eye, and also desirable for gaining wisdom, she took some and ate it" (Gen 3:6a)—but that comes sometime (who knows how long?) after her reply to the serpent.[24] How can one know that she gives the forbidden object her attention in a concentrated way

---

24. It is another interesting, but unanswerable, question, how long it took for the serpent to bring the woman down—i.e., to the point one reads in Gen 3:6. C. S. Lewis offered intriguing insight into this question in his novel *Perelandra*. In that story, Satan, who had possessed a British physicist who had voyaged to Venus, tries to tempt the Venusian "Eve" to disobey the Lord's one command: that neither she nor her husband should leave their floating island home and travel to the mainland. In Lewis's story, Satan takes days of endless argument to wear the woman down and—almost—bring her around to his point of view, but ultimately he fails. By creating such a story, Lewis exposed an issue never addressed by commentators: Just how long did it take the serpent to produce the result he desired in our first mother? No one can answer the question, but kudos to Lewis for raising it. Cf. C. S. Lewis, *Perelandra* (New York: Macmillan, 1944), 108–94.

when she answers the serpent's question in Genesis
3:2–3?

One might argue that, with Ross as with other interpreters
considered up to this point, there is a fundamental but virtually
unspoken problem when it comes to interpreting Genesis 3:2–3. The
problem is: How does one understand sin? If "whatever is not of
faith is sin"—that is, whatever does not completely amen the Lord
and agree with what he is, says, and does—then it would be impossible that Adam had misinformed his wife and equally impossible
that his wife added to what the Lord had said. If either were true,
Adam or his wife would be sinning already, and Paul would have
been mistaken when he wrote, "it was the woman who was *deceived
and became a sinner*" (1 Tim 2:14, emphasis added; cf. Gen 3:13b, "The
serpent deceived me, and I ate").

Ross has also noted that the woman "used the serpent's designation" of "God," rather than "the Lord." This is a noteworthy
observation, but what does it imply? It would appear to suggest the
woman is drifting toward the serpent's view of things at this stage of
the conversation, since she uses his name, "God," rather than "the
Lord" or "the Lord God" (per Genesis 2, in which the Lord God was
dealing with Adam and created the woman). There is a preferable
way to see it, however, and it has to do with the use of the divine
names "Yahweh" and "God" in Genesis. That usage apparently has
to do with the covenant relationship in view in the context in which
the name is used. But first, one should note that the woman's reply
could be seen as a natural reply to someone (the serpent) who has
just spoken, using his own term for God, which of course is no ille-
gitimate term. But this is where the use of divine names in Genesis
becomes important for understanding why the woman refers to the
Lord as "God" when she answers the serpent. The woman is in a
personal covenantal relationship with the Lord [יהוה] who had given

her covenantal responsibilities (Gen 1:28–29), and the name Yahweh ("the Lord") appears first in the Lord's detailed dealings with the humans in Genesis 2.[25] The serpent is in no such relationship. It was therefore appropriate for the woman to use the serpent's term for the creator God, because the serpent as a lower creature stood only in that more general relationship to God [אלהים, "Elohim"; Gen 1:1]. We will take up this matter in more detail in the following chapter.

Ross notes further that, by giving her simple and sinless paraphrase of what the Lord said about dying, the woman may have left herself—innocently, naively—in a condition in which the warning would lose some of its force:

> The changes that were made between this verse and the giving of the commandment are within the legitimate range of interpretation. There is no violation in free paraphrasing of the words of the Lord. However, if the precise wording of the original commandment is weakened, the appeal to sin grows stronger. "Lest you die" carries the meaning of God's warning, but it does not clearly retain the certainty of the penalty of death. As Westermann commented, "A command that is questioned is no longer the original command" [*Genesis*, vol. 1, p. 239].[26]

One might counter, however, that as we are dealing with a paraphrase, the admonition "lest you die" is forceful enough. It may be true that the woman's report of the Lord's warning could entail some ambiguity and thus would "not clearly retain the certainty of the penalty of death." Nonetheless, as we have noted, the adverb

---

25. The compound name "the Lord God" or "Yahweh God" apparently equates to "the Lord [is] God," or "Yahweh [is] Elohim," like, e.g., "Amon Ra ("Amon [is] Ra") in Egypt. So, in Genesis 2, it informs the reader that Yahweh, in personal covenantal relationship with the man and woman, is the "God" ("Elohim") of Genesis 1.

26. Ross, *Creation and Blessing*, 135.

used can indicate the certainty of an event, and there is no evidence that the woman's paraphrase was meant to introduce ambiguity, nor that she had begun to doubt the certainty of death in her own thoughts.[27] Westermann's comment ("A command that is questioned is no longer the original command") has been discussed above. It could be that the woman's paraphrase has somehow, in her own mind, weakened the force of what the Lord had said, although there is no proof that her paraphrase affected her in that way and thus helped pave her way to sin. Moreover, there is no statement or proof that the woman is in any way questioning the Lord's command when she answers the serpent's question.

G. K. BEALE

Recently G. K. Beale, following Ross, has gone into more detail on the matter:

> When confronted by the satanic serpent, Adam's wife responds by quoting Gen 2:16–17 but changes the wording in at least three major places (Gen 3:2–3). It is possible that the changes are incidental and are a mere paraphrase still retaining the same meaning as in 2:16–17. It is more likely, however, that she either failed to remember God's word accurately or intentionally changed it for her own purposes. The telltale sign of this is that each change appears to have theological significance. First, she minimizes their privileges by saying merely, "We may eat," whereas God had said, "You may eat freely"; second, she minimizes the judgment by saying, "You will die," whereas God had said, "You will surely die"; third, she maximizes the prohibition by

---

27. Cf. Ps 2:12, "Kiss the Son, lest (פֶּן) He be angry / And you perish in the way" (NKJV) and discussion of Calvin above.

affirming, "You shall ... not touch," whereas God had originally said only, "You shall not eat."[28]

Beale follows Ross's rather negative—or, as I have suggested,
prosecutorial—view of the matter: "Adam's wife ... changes the
wording" of what God said "in at least three major places." One
could, nonetheless, suggest a more neutral statement: "Adam's
wife ... briefly summarized." Beyond the limited data of Genesis
3:2–3, however, it is worth remembering that the Bible nowhere
faults the woman for the infractions that have been named, if
they are infractions, but only says she was deceived and became a
sinner (1 Tim 2:14). Moreover, as has been noted, even if she "failed
to remember God's word accurately" she would have been in sin
already, because already she would not have amened—faithfully
represented—God at precisely that point.[29] *Whatever* is not of faith
is sin.

Beale's negative evaluation of each of the woman's comments is
of course no personal idiosyncrasy. It is true to the tradition under
review. The final point of agreement with that tradition is the understanding that the woman *adds* ("You shall not touch") *to what God
had said*. As this work proposes, what has been characterized as
her addition can reasonably—and possibly better—be accounted
for by the laconic nature of this early narrative material (much like
Abraham's later "addition" when he explained his ruse to Abimelek;
Gen 20:13).[30] A preferable view of the woman's statements therefore
might eschew terms like "minimizes" and "maximizes" because
they characterize the woman's words in ways that cannot be unambiguously substantiated from the text. They imply a motivation

---

28. G. K. Beale, *New Testament Biblical Theology* (Grand Rapids: Baker Academic,
2011), 33. Cf. similarly Gordon Wenham, *Genesis 1–15*, WBC 1 (Waco, TX: Word, 1987), 75.

29. Cf. discussion of this issue in chapter 1.

30. As is discussed in chapter 4; cf. Niehaus, *BT* 2, 99n19.

that has not been demonstrated and, as has been seen, cannot be demonstrated because of the laconic nature of the material. Any claim of motive can only make sense (and yet *cannot be proved*) if it turns out that the woman added to God's original command rather than simply giving further information about it. In that case, some motive would naturally have to be sought (although one could never really be sure that one had found the right motive) to account for her adding to what God had said. Again, the evidence may invite speculation, but it does not offer proof.

The characterization espoused by Ross and more recently Beale elaborates in greater detail an understanding held for centuries by many. It has the virtue of elaboration—of developing an older view perhaps as much as it can be developed. But, like the work of prior interpreters, it does not appear to take into account the true nature of sin (per Rom 14:23b).

I here propose, then, that the woman was not in sin before she was "deceived and *became* a sinner," because there is no biblical evidence that she was in sin before that moment. Paul says that first, she was deceived; then, she became a sinner. She did not first minimize or maximize what God had said "for her own purposes," for then she would already have been a sinner, having failed to represent God faithfully in these crucial matters. (Moreover, one should ask, what were "her own purposes"?[31]) It is important to remember that at this point in the narrative the serpent has not tempted or deceived her. He has only asked, "Did God really say, 'You must not eat from any tree in the garden?'" (Gen 3:1b). The woman then answers his question. If her answer shows that her purposes were to take the fruit and eat it—or if she had any purposes related to

---

31. Beale does not explain what he means by this intriguing phrase, but if the "purposes" were "her *own* purposes," then, as this contrastive expression seems to indicate, they were apparently not God's purposes.

the fruit that were her own and contrary to God's—then she already purposed or knowingly intended sin, and Paul was mistaken when he wrote, "The woman ... was *deceived* and *became* a sinner" (1 Tim 2:14, emphasis added).[32]

I propose the following as a view that takes into account Paul's evaluation and his definition of sin: the woman gave the serpent a brief but sufficient précis of what God said about eating from the other trees and about dying should she and her husband transgress. But when it came to the all-important injunction (Gen 2:17b; Gen 3:3b), she gave a fuller account of it for the serpent's benefit, and (as it turns out) for the benefit of those who subsequently read Genesis 2–3: they were forbidden not only to eat the fruit from the tree but even to touch the tree.

We turn now to a handful of evangelical views that do not fit seamlessly into the traditional fabric of evangelical interpretation. Nonetheless, they mostly agree that the woman added to what God had said.

JAMES MURPHY AND R. PAYNE SMITH

A couple of nineteenth-century scholars did not adopt the usual view. James Murphy supposed the woman did add to what the Lord God had said but nonetheless had not started to go astray at that point; R. Payne Smith thought the woman did not add to what the Lord God had said. Both arguments in favor of the woman's innocence appear to have certain weaknesses.

James G. Murphy argued, in a way that some might see as very generous, for the woman's simplicity and sincerity:

---

32. Moreover, if even fallen humans under the new covenant are those who "take captive every thought to make it obedient to Christ" (2 Cor 10:5), and if the new covenant is aimed at restoring all things, any thought at variance with God's intent before the fall would have been sin (i.e., disobedience in her thoughts) and again, the woman is never faulted for having her own purposes before she was tempted.

> The woman gives the natural and distinct answer of unaf-
> fected sincerity to this suggestion. The deviations from the
> strict letter of the law are nothing more than the free and
> earnest expressions of her feelings. The expression, "nei-
> ther shall ye touch it," merely implies that they were not to
> meddle with it, as a forbidden thing.[33]

However, to say that deviations from the letter of the law are not
sin might entail difficulties. A free and earnest expression of feelings, however sincere, may still be sin. After all, one may be sincere
and yet mistaken. If Christ has come to restore all things, and if
Christians are exhorted to take every thought captive to obey him,
one might expect that the woman, as yet untainted by sin, could,
and should, have done the same. Her departure from the law, for
whatever reason, would still be sin. One might also recall the statement: "For whoever keeps the whole law and yet stumbles at just
one point is guilty of breaking all of it" (Jas 2:10)—a statement con-
cordant with Paul's explanation, "Whatever is not from faith is sin."
Whatever does not amen God—and that would include adding to
what God had said and attributing the additions to him—is sin.

R. Payne Smith also apparently but in a rather different way did
not see her answer as sin: "Eve, *who at first had answered rightly*, and
who as yet knew nothing of falsehood, dallied with the temptation,
and was lost" (emphasis added).[34] Payne Smith seems to mean that

---

33. James G. Murphy, *A Critical and Exegetical Commentary on the Book of Genesis, with a New Translation* (Boston: Estes and Lauriat, 1873), 112. It appears that Murphy's concern with the woman's feelings and sincerity is characteristic of what has been called the Romantic era (i.e., from the late 18th to the late 19th century) and its empha-sis on individual feeling and imagination—itself rooted in the perceived importance of sentiment and sincerity that grew in England in the late 18th century. Cf. Walter Jackson Bate, *From Classic to Romantic: Premises of Taste in Eighteenth Century England* (Cambridge: Harvard University Press, 1946).

34. R. Payne Smith, *Genesis* (London: Cassel & Co., Ltd., 1885), 93.

the woman's *answer* was entirely right (i.e., in vv. 2–3) but then afterward she "dallied with the temptation" when she considered the tree more closely (i.e., in Gen 3:6a) and as a result entered into sin (in Gen 3:6b). If there is a weakness in this statement it would be that it might have been developed with more detail and to better effect. Nonetheless, this view appears to concur with the view taken in the present work and with 1 Timothy 2:14.

BASIL F. C. ATKINSON: AN INTERPRETATION, NOT AN ADDITION

Basil Atkinson, a mid-twentieth-century evangelical scholar, attempted to salvage the woman's reply to the serpent by saying she did not add to what God had said but only interpreted it:

> *Neither shall ye touch.* Eve has been accused of adding to the word of God by the utterance of this phrase, but the charge is not necessarily just. She may have been interpreting the prohibition, and her interpretation seems a sensible one. There was no object in touching the tree, and it would obviously be safer not to do so. The man and woman seem wisely to have decided not to go near the tree. If fallen sinners today were only to give temptation as wide a berth as this, there would be less tragedy in the world.[35]

"There was no object in touching the tree, and it would obviously be safer not to do so." One might surmise, however, that it was precisely for this reason that the Lord told Adam in Genesis 2 not even to touch the tree, as his wife subsequently reported in Genesis 3:3. No doubt such a stricture, whether imposed by the Lord or self-imposed by Adam and his wife, would be the better part of discretion. Although that is true, the account does not provide the

---

35. Basil F. C. Atkinson, *The Book of Genesis* (Chicago: Moody Press, 1957), 42.

information that Adam and his wife "wisely ... decided not to go near the tree," and there is unfortunately no evidence in this passage or later in the Bible that they made this decision. Additionally, what if the woman did attribute to God something he had not said, "and you shall not touch it"? One might reasonably question how that could be an interpretation of the command, "You shall not eat of it." (It is important not to lose sight of the fact that she did not offer those words as her own interpretation, but as something God had said.) Regrettably, if she was interpreting what the Lord had said, or what the Lord had intended, or even what his command implied, we are not told those things by the text.

P. WAYNE TOWNSEND: AN ATTEMPT TO SALVAGE THE WOMAN'S "ADDITION"

Among evangelical scholars there is one attempt that stands out for its uniqueness as an effort to validate what the woman says in Genesis 3:3, and it deserves special attention. P. Wayne Townsend has made a novel effort to account for the woman's reply to the serpent.[36] He argues, "Eve's statements might be original to the story and indicative of the story's dependence on the cleanness code found in Leviticus 11."[37] Townsend proposes that Genesis, as a document written for people in Moses' day and later, depended on the Mosaic law that came much later for certain ideas, phrases, and concepts.[38] Laudable as the effort appears to be, it may not take

---

36. P. Wayne Townsend, "Eve's Answer to the Serpent: An Alternative Paradigm for Sin and Some Implications in Theology," *CTJ* 33 (1998): 399–420.

37. Townsend, "Eve's Answer," 405.

38. E.g., Townsend, "Eve's Answer," 403, affirms: "In this context, the story of the Fall functions as a pretext for the exodus-conquest. Genesis 3 identifies the sources of evil that have led to the suffering of slavery. It also justifies the conquest by expanding the division between the woman and the Serpent to an ongoing struggle between their descendants (Gen 3:15). All of this relies on a separation from, and over against, the rest of the nations—the very separation identified in the Levitical code (Lev 18:24–30; 20:22–27)."

the passage seriously enough as history. The account in Genesis 2–3, however laconic it is, purports to be a narrative of what actually happened—rather than a story (even written by Moses) that uses later concepts from the Mosaic law to create a Genesis narrative that in some ways anticipates Israel's later history.

Townsend proposes that the phrase "you shall not touch it" comes from the realm of Levitical law. After arguing for the dependence of concepts in Genesis on the subsequent Pentateuch he says:

> Given such a dependence, the phrase, "do not touch," functions to draw the readers' attention beyond the bounds of Genesis itself and into the cleanness code. As I will show shortly, it raises in the mind of the original reader many associations that enrich the meaning of the text and communicate more than our present tradition of commentary suggests.
>
> With this understanding, we may revisit the words of Eve to the Serpent. She specifies that "God did say ... you may not touch it [the fruit]" (Gen 3:3). If we restrict the context of these words to Genesis, then we must admit that God did not say that (Gen 2:17). But, if we allow that the writer of Genesis expected a basic familiarity with the law of Sinai, we must allow a broader context for this statement, including the Sinai laws found in the whole Pentateuch. In this broader context the words, "you may not touch," take on deeper significance.[39]

It turns out, then, that Townsend regards the command not to touch the tree ("you must not touch it," Gen 3:3) as something God did not in fact say: "If we restrict the context of these words to Genesis, then we must admit that God did not say that (Gen 2:17)." For Townsend that is not a problem, however, because the point of the story is that

---

39. Townsend, "Eve's Answer," 406.

readers understand it in terms of later pentateuchal injunctions that informed its composition:

> We find parallels to Eve's words in Leviticus 11 and Deuteronomy 14. Leviticus 11 defines food that is lawful for Israelites to eat. Concerning unclean land animals, verse 8 states, "You must not *eat* their meat or *touch* their carcasses; they are unclean for you" (emphasis added). The vocabulary and sentence structure of this verse strongly parallels Eve's words in Genesis 3:3: "You must not eat fruit ... and you must not touch it."[40]

Townsend proceeds to cite examples from Leviticus and Deuteronomy.[41] He reasons: "Read in this light, the original readers of Genesis 3 would have understood Eve's words as a natural

---

40. Townsend, "Eve's Answer," 406.

41. Townsend, "Eve's Answer," 406: "This parallel strengthens when we realize that this is a special prohibition against touching unclean (forbidden) food and is beyond the prohibition against touching dead clean animals given in Leviticus 11:39–40. Furthermore, this combined prohibition against eating *and* touching repeats throughout the chapter (with certain stylistic variations) in reference to various forbidden foods. Indeed, the prohibition against touching becomes a crescendo of emphasis as the chapter proceeds: unclean water creatures—'And since you are to detest them, you must not eat their meat and you must detest their carcasses' (v. 11); flying creatures—'These are the birds you are to detest and not eat because they are detestable [to you] ... whoever touches their carcasses will be unclean till evening' (vv. 13, 24b); land animals (again!)—'whoever touches the carcasses of any of them will be unclean ... whoever touches their carcasses will be unclean until evening. Anyone who picks up their carcasses must wash his clothes, and he will be unclean until evening' (26b, 27b–28a).

"Deuteronomy 14:8b repeats this pattern once, phrasing the prohibition identically to Leviticus 11:8a, the closest Leviticus parallel to Genesis 3:3. While it could be argued that Deuteronomy 14 was derived from Leviticus 11, such a derivation does not lessen the strength of the parallel to Genesis 3:3. The very choice of this phrase over others in Leviticus 11, whether by derivation or common source, points to it as a key phrase in teaching the prohibitions against unclean food." It should be noted that God gave the Sinai covenant material through Moses and then later also the legal renewal of that material in the Moab covenant (Deuteronomy) through Moses, so there is no need to raise the question, "whether by derivation or common source," regarding the relationship of Deuteronomy 14 to Leviticus 11.

outgrowth of God's command in Genesis 2:17. The Tree of the
Knowledge of Good and Evil was forbidden food, and therefore
unclean."[42]

Because the proposed Levitical background explains the woman's famous addition, related temple and worship matters are also
implied, despite admitted dietary differences between humanity's
first parents and the Israelites under Moses:

> Obviously there are differences. Israel knew of no unclean
> plants or fruit. But then, Adam and Eve did not eat meat; fruit
> was the extent of the food granted (Gen. 2:16). Furthermore,
> the consequences of even touching the fruit of the Tree of
> the Knowledge of Good and Evil was death (Gen. 3:3), while
> touching unclean food only made one unclean until eve-
> ning (Lev. 11:24–28). Yet the consequences of even temporary
> uncleanness were severe. It required a sin offering for atone-
> ment (Lev. 5:2, 5–6), and cut one off from worship, requiring
> death for the unclean worshiper (Lev. 7:21 cf. Ex. 31:14 for
> the meaning of the phrase "cut off"). Following Meredith
> G. Kline, the Garden of Eden was a holy temple-garden,
> the temple (I Kings 6:23–35). Such an understanding would
> equate any unclean person in the Garden of Eden with an
> unclean person in the temple or even the Holy of Holies—a
> situation demanding death. But even if we ignore such a
> connection between the garden and temple, if an Israelite
> ate unclean food and did not cleanse himself, the ominous
> threat is proclaimed "he will be held responsible" (Lev. 17:16).
> And eating unclean food was a sin that subjected the whole
> nation to exile (Lev. 20:22–26), an obvious parallel to the
> punishment of Adam and Eve.[43]

---

42. Townsend, "Eve's Answer," 406–7.
43. Townsend, "Eve's Answer," 407.

The Eden-temple connection is one that Kline championed and others have affirmed. I have also agreed with it. Nonetheless, Townsend arguably has reconstructed the whole matter in precisely the opposite direction to what one would naturally understand, given the chronological ordering of the biblical data. Just as the first temple (Eden) preceded the tabernacle, the Jerusalem temple, and the church, so the idea of neither eating nor touching originated in Eden. It was not read back—or composed back—into the Eden scenario when Genesis 2 and 3 were written, not even by Moses. Rather, Genesis 2 and 3 report what happened and what was said. Such realities as we find in Genesis 3 would play out under the Mosaic covenant quite naturally in sinful ways in a fallen world: there would be, by God's definition, clean and unclean foods, penalties for eating and touching them, desecration of the tabernacle/temple, and eventually exile.[44]

Before departing from Townsend's ingenious effort, we should note that he draws another conclusion that, although it may be unlikely, is based on a very old understanding of Genesis 3:8:

> Finally, we must reckon with the repeated emphasis on evening. Temporary uncleanness by touching demanded immediate cleansing and left one unclean until evening (Lev. 11:25, 28, 31, 32, 39, 40; 17:15). Could this be why Genesis 3:8 notes that God came walking in the "cool of the day," that is, after sunset? Does the narrative indicate that God is visiting them after the time when their uncleanness should have been cleansed, a time when the offense of uncleanness should normally have passed?[45]

---

44. For comment on the parallel between the Adamic expulsion from Eden and Israel's later exile, and the fact that neither event means abrogation of the respective covenants (i.e., Adamic or Mosaic), cf. Niehaus, *BT* 2, 11.

45. Townsend, "Eve's Answer," 407.

Some years ago I argued for—and since have reaffirmed—an alternate translation for the traditional "in the cool of the day"—namely, "in the wind of the storm."[46] This translation, based on cognate evidence from Akkadian, appears to be gaining some traction.[47] It reflects a better understanding than the ancient guess, made by the Septuagint translators, that has been repeated ever since. Granted this new understanding, one could affirm that evening had nothing to do with what happened in Genesis 3. But even if the Lord did come "in the cool of the day," and even if that meant he came in the evening (*instead of the morning, which would also be cool!*), the information would not tell us the Lord visited them "after the time when their uncleanness should have been cleansed, a time when the offense of uncleanness should normally have passed." Why would such an idea have any meaning to Adam and his wife in Eden? There is unfortunately no evidence that a concept of uncleanness, from which they should be cleansed before sunset, had any place in their thoughts, because no such concept is mentioned in Genesis 2–3, which I take as an account of what was actually said and done. The Lord promised death if they violated his command. He made no mention either of uncleanness or of any way they might be cleansed of it. Finally: even if we take the narrative in the rather fictional sense Townsend intends—even if these nuances had been made part of the *story* (say, by Moses) for the benefit of later readers—those later, thoughtful readers might naturally wonder why

---

46. Jeffrey J. Niehaus, "In the Wind of the Storm: Another Look at Genesis III 8," *VT* 44.2 (1994): 263–67; Niehaus, *God at Sinai* (Grand Rapids: Zondervan, 1995), 155–59; *BT* 1, 105–6.

47. Cf. John Walton, *The IVP Bible Background Commentary: Genesis–Deuteronomy* (Downers Grove, IL: InterVarsity Press, 1997), 32; David J. A. Clines and John Elwolde, eds., *Yodh-Lamedh*, vol. 4 of *The Dictionary of Classical Hebrew* (Sheffield: Sheffield Academic Press, 1998), 185.

such ideas would matter in the Eden story itself, since the Lord had not said anything about them in Genesis 2–3.

I cannot agree therefore with Townsend's effort to account for the woman's words, "and you may not touch it." He has suggested, "Eve's statements might be original to the story and indicative of the story's dependence on the cleanness code found in Leviticus 11." According to Townsend's reconstruction, then, the woman apparently never said those words. They are simply attributed to her by the author of Genesis as part of the story in order to make a point about uncleanness for readers of his own time:

> In light of all of this one can argue that the original read-ers of Eve's words would have understood the story in the context of God's commands concerning unclean foods, and would have understood that the fruit of the Tree of the Knowledge of Good and Evil was unclean food. This has consequences for ... our reading of Genesis 3.[48]

The approach taken by Townsend is ingenious, but one may wonder whether it does more harm than good. It does not actu-ally read Genesis 2 and 3 as historical accounts. It reads them as literary creations—effectively, fictions—in a well-intended sense, whose purpose is to show something about primal sin in terms later readers would understand. They would understand, because the narrative was meant to remind them concerning what God later revealed to Israel, not to tell them about God's primordial interac-tions with Adam and his wife. In sum: the historical retrojection undermines the historicity of the Genesis account and makes it

---

48. Townsend, "Eve's Answer," 407.

an instructional product of and for a later age; it becomes a story meant to tell something about sin.[49]

The approach, then, would appear to take away more than it gives. It would seem better to accept the events of Genesis 2 and 3 as historical facts, as, for instance, Jesus and Paul did (e.g., Matt 19:4–6; 1 Tim 2:13–14). Taken as such, they show that human disobedience from the beginning had characteristics that would recur in God's dealings with his people because our fallen nature does not change.

SUMMARY COMMENTS

A long tradition has maintained that, in Genesis 3:3b, the woman added to what God said in Genesis 2:17b. Notable exponents of this tradition are Martin Luther, C. F. Keil, F. Delitzsch, Geerhardus Vos, and Meredith Kline. A different and perhaps more circumspect understanding of Genesis 3:1–6, especially of verse 3b, is proposed here—namely, that the woman did not add to what the Lord God had said but instead supplied further information to the laconic account in Genesis 2. If this understanding is correct, it may navigate past what would then be two problems one could identify in the long tradition of interpretation that has been reviewed.

FIRST PROBLEM: COMMENTS ON THE WOMAN

The first interpretive problem is a very understandable desire to understand the woman's psychological state when she answers

---

49. One could wish that Townsend had done more to distinguish what might be actual history in Genesis 2–3 and what might be purely literary creation, but he does not explore that topic in any focused way. His emphasis seems to be on the legal/theological purpose of the story. To the extent that he discusses what did or did not happen, he does so with reference to the context of the story (e.g., "If we restrict the context of these words to Genesis, then we must admit that God did not say that"), but he is not clear about whether any of these events ever took place in an absolute, historical sense.

the serpent's question. Regrettably, the text of Genesis 3:2–3 does not give us this information. Precisely because the narrative of Genesis 2–3 is so laconic, it is impossible to know what is going on in the woman's mind (at least, until we are told, in verse 6). Consequently the traditional interpretation, in its several nuanced iterations, cannot offer beyond a reasonable doubt an analysis of the woman's state of mind or feelings. It would seem that efforts to understand her inner state from the few words she says can only be speculative and inconclusive.[50]

SECOND PROBLEM: LACK OF COMPARATIVE STUDY

The second problem is also methodological. When one compares Genesis 3:2–3 with Genesis 2:17, one is actually comparing a type of narrative sequence: a first-person account of an event with a prior third-person omniscient account of that event. It might be helpful to see if other narratives in Genesis offer material for similar comparisons. Analysis of other evidence might provide guidelines or controls when one returns to Genesis 2–3 to see what conclusions are warranted. However, in the interpretive tradition engaged in this chapter, whether the commentators have come from the liberal or conservative side of the interpretive spectrum, no one—inexplicably, as it would seem—has taken the pattern of differences between the third-person "omniscient" account of Genesis 2:17 and the first-person recounting in Genesis 3:2–3 and compared it with other examples of the same sort of narrative sequence elsewhere

---

50. Cf. Henry Alford, *The Book of Genesis* (Minneapolis: Kirk & Kirk, 1872), 15. Long ago, Alford warned about "the insecurity of such fine tracking of words to their supposed sources. The same may be said of almost all the minute inferences which scholars have drawn from the woman's reply [i.e., in Gen 3:2–3]. The best exposure of their unsafeness is that some hold Eve's reply to be a sign of her unswerving loyalty, others of her incipient disloyalty to God."

in Genesis or in the Bible. The same is true of the earlier (i.e., pre-critical) history of interpretation.

A comparison of that sort could be helpful, and there are two very suitable Old Testament examples: Moses' Genesis 12 account of Abram's ruse as compared with Abraham's later accounting of it in Genesis 20, and Moses' portrayal of the Lord's interactions with Abram/Abraham in Genesis 12–22 as compared with the Lord's summary in Genesis 26:5 of the commands and requirements he communicated to Abraham. As noted in the introduction to the present work, one New Testament exemplar will also receive consideration: Luke's Acts 9 account of Paul's Damascus road experience as compared with Paul's later recounting of it in Acts 22 and Acts 26. The value of the Genesis examples could be that they would show the same historiographical technique used by one author, Moses. The value of the Acts examples could be that they would show a pattern of reporting in the New Testament consistent with what has been documented (in three well-known cases) in the Old Testament.

Comparative study of these narrative sequences appears to support the point made about the woman's seeming changes and addition to what is reported in Genesis 2. The divine account noted in Genesis 26:5 and considered vis-à-vis the earlier Abrahamic-covenant narrative material in Genesis 12–22 makes the point perhaps with even greater force than any of the other examples, since it is the Lord himself who is supplying the additional information. The differences between the first, historian's account of these matters and the later, individual's/Yahweh's recounting of them, recorded by the historian in each case, is an understandable part of narrative technique and shows how laconic each initial account is. The recurrence of this reportorial pattern would suggest that it does not matter—historiographically speaking—whether the individual involved is the woman before the fall, Abram/Abraham in a fallen state before and after the cutting of the Abrahamic covenant, the Lord himself, or Paul before and after his conversion. The salient point would be that the historian in each case gives a laconic account of an event and then reports how an individual later recounted it and supplied more information in doing so. A commitment to seeing the issue from this point of view—that is, seeing it as a matter of narrative art conveying historical sequences—can go far to help avoid imputing to the woman a fault for which the Lord himself is never reported as rebuking her, or seeing sin in her before the serpent deceived her and she ate.

4

OTHER BIBLICAL ACCOUNTS

I have proposed that when the woman answered the serpent's question in Genesis 3 and said God told them not to eat from *or touch* the tree of the knowledge of good and evil, she did not add to what God had said but actually reported what God had said. Umberto Cassuto is one of the very few scholars who noted this possibility, but he rejected it: "This hypothesis is improbable, for the exact nature of the prohibition should have been precisely formulated when the Lord God spoke to the man."[1] Cassuto's sense of things would seem to be indisputable in this regard. Unlike Bonhoeffer, who thought God said things to Adam that Adam could not have understood, Cassuto reasons that the Lord God would have communicated to Adam exactly what he needed to know: and so, the Lord God *did* formulate the prohibition precisely.[2] The question at the moment, however, is whether Moses, the historian, reported what the Lord God said in toto in Genesis 2:17 or whether he reserved the fuller revelation of what the Lord had said and included it in

---

1. Umberto Cassuto, *A Commentary on the Book of Genesis, Part One: From Adam to Noah, Gen I–VI 8*, trans. Israel Abrahams (Jerusalem: Magnes, 1961), 145.

2. For discussion of Bonhoeffer's comments, see chapter 1.

the woman's report later (specifically, in Genesis 3:3b). How can one resolve this question—or at least provide a resolution that is more likely to be correct than other solutions that have been proposed?[3]

METHODOLOGICAL
CONSIDERATIONS (REPRISE)

Beyond a study of Genesis 2–3 *in isolation* (i.e., without regard to potential comparative evidence beyond those chapters), one way to help resolve the question would be to find other examples of the same phenomenon later in the Bible. If other biblical narratives—especially within Genesis—provide parallel cases, they could provide evidence for or against the view of Genesis 2–3 taken in the present work.

As has been suggested, other biblical cases of reported speech do apparently show a kindred pattern of laconic third-person reporting of an event supplemented by a later first-person account of the same event. Two other examples from Genesis invite the consideration that Moses used a method of laconic reporting and later supplementation more than once. One example involves reported human speech. The other example involves reported divine speech. A human example (Gen 12, 20) and a divine example from the Abrahamic covenant narratives (Gen 12–22) and Genesis 26:5 can

---

3. Nearly two and a half centuries ago John Gill anticipated the explanation set forth and advocated at greater length in the present work: "God hath said, ye shall not eat of it, neither shall ye touch it, lest ye die: here the woman is charged by some both with adding to, and taking from the law of God; and if so, *must have sinned very heinously before she eat of the fruit*; but neither of them are sufficiently proved; not the former by her saying, 'neither shall ye touch it,' which though not expressed in the prohibition, is implied, namely, such a touching the fruit as to pluck it off the tree, take it in the hand, and put it to the mouth, in order to eat it" (emphasis added). The present work argues however that the woman's "additional" words do not merely draw out the implications of what the Lord said but report more fully what he said. Cf. John Gill, *An Exposition of the First Book of Moses Called Genesis* (1778, 1810; repr., Springfield: Particular Baptist Press, 2010), 53.

shed light on Moses' compositional technique and also fortify the
view proffered here regarding the woman's response to the serpent.[4]

INTRODUCTORY REVIEW OF GENESIS 2:16–17 AND 3:2–3

Before we turn to those cases, a comparative review of what the Lord
God said in Genesis 2 and the woman's report of it in Genesis 3 is in
order. The following display will facilitate comparison:

The Historian's Account of What the Lord God Said

2:16   The LORD *God commanded* [ויצו יהוה אלהים]
          the man:

          "*You are free to eat* [אכל תאכל] from *any tree*
          in the garden [מכל עץ הגן]

2:17   but you must not eat from the tree *of the
          knowledge of good and evil,*

          for when you eat from it you will certainly die
          [מות תמות]."

The Woman's Recounting of What God Said

3:2   "*We may eat* [נאכל] *fruit* from *the trees* in the
          garden [מפרי עץ הגן],

3:3   but *God did say* [אמר אלהים], 'You must not
          eat fruit from the tree *that is in the middle of
          the garden, and you must not touch it,* or you
          will die [lit., "lest you die," פן תמתון]."

---

4. In the New Testament a comparison of Luke's account of Paul's Damascus road
experience and Paul's own later accounts of it, first before the crowd in Jerusalem
and then before Festus and Agrippa (recorded in Acts 9, 22, and 26 respectively)
will illustrate the same compositional technique used by the historian in the New
Testament. Study of the Lukan materials is reserved for the following chapter.

I have given the Hebrew for terms that are especially important in the narrative. The following italicized differences are noteworthy: (1) Genesis 2:16 says, "The LORD God *commanded* the man,"
whereas Genesis 3:3 says "but *God did say*." (2) Genesis 2:17a says,
"but you must not eat from the tree *of the knowledge of good and evil*,"
whereas Genesis 3:3 says, "You must not eat fruit from the tree *that
is in the middle of the garden, and you must not touch it*." (3) Genesis
2:17b says "*you will surely die*," whereas Genesis 3:3b says "*you will*
[lit., 'lest you'] *die*."[5]

It will be good not to lose sight of a point made by Alford and
elaborated in the previous chapter: interpreters are not in a position to know what the woman was thinking in Genesis 3:3, however natural the desire to do so may be. The concern can only be,
appropriately and in the first instance, with the verbal content of
her response to the serpent in the context of Genesis 2–3. It has
been noted that, apart from her seeming addition of the words,
"and you must not touch it," the woman's account of what God had
said could be a paraphrase of the essentials. When the woman says,
"We may eat fruit from the trees in the garden" (Gen 3:3a), as contrasted with "you are free to eat from any tree in the garden" (Gen
2:16b), she may not be diminishing the Lord's blessing. After all, if
they may eat from the trees in the garden (as the woman says without any stated limitation), then they are ipso facto free to eat "from
any tree" in the garden—with the one exception that the woman
goes on to explain. When she says, "God did say," instead of "the
LORD God commanded," she is not necessarily diminishing the
force of the earlier report. If God says not to do something, he is
commanding one not to do it. When she says, "The tree ... in the
middle of the garden," instead of "the tree of the knowledge of good
and evil," she is not altering anything; she is simply locating the

_____

5. Cf. chapters 2 and 3 for discussion of the force of the expression "lest you die."

forbidden tree as the narrator had done before in Genesis 2:9b ("In the middle of the garden [was] … the tree of the knowledge of good and evil"). When she says God said, "You will die," instead of "you will certainly die," this again appears to be a distinction without a difference if we consider who is giving the warning (namely, God). If God says you will die, then you will surely die. The woman uses a less forceful statement in her summary of the main points, but that need not create a problem. She does not owe the serpent an account of God's ipsissima verba. Finally, the issue here is whether a compelling case can be made that she is diminishing, for whatever reason, the blessing and the curse. One cannot insist upon this as long as a reasonable alternative is available: she gives the serpent a summary account, which is not verbatim but which also, as an overall summary, has no inaccuracies.

It is germane to return at this point to an observation by Allen Ross: "She added to the prohibition. The Lord had said nothing about touching the tree, but Eve said that God [she used the serpent's designation] said, 'Neither shall you touch it.'"[6] Ross notes that she "used the serpent's designation." The implication would seem to be that her use of the serpent's term for God suggests she was already coming under his influence. It is possible, however, that she used the serpent's choice of divine name for a very good reason. God (אלהים, "Elohim," Gen 3:3) created the cosmos (Gen 1:1), but Yahweh was in personal relationship with his covenant vassals, Adam and his wife. How should that fact affect one's understanding of the woman's reply to the serpent? When the woman referred to the deity as "God" and not "Yahweh [the Lord]," or as "Yahweh God," she was responding to the serpent with the term the serpent had used (אלהים, "God") not because she was already coming under

---

6. Allen P. Ross, *Creation and Blessing: A Guide to the Study and Exposition of the Book of Genesis* (Grand Rapids: Baker Academic, 1988), 134–35.

the serpent's influence and following his lead but because Elohim ("God") was the appropriate designation for deity as far as the serpent was concerned—as a creature not made in the *imago Dei* and not in the same personal covenantal relationship with the Lord.[7] The serpent used the term for God as the serpent knew him, and the woman also used the term for God appropriate to a creature lower in the order of creation (a serpent).

Interpreters have not exactly faulted the woman for contradicting God, but they have sometimes come close. It may be a helpful distinction that the woman did not contradict what the Lord God had said but paraphrased it. The Bible contains other paraphrases, as the comparison of Luke's account of Paul's Damascus road experience and Paul's retellings of it will show, and it is important to remember that the Bible nowhere faults the woman for answering the serpent's question the way she did. But what, then, of her seeming addition to what God said?

As a stepping-stone to the comparisons that follow, a reiteration of the perspective taken here may be useful. As has been noted, reporting is almost inevitably laconic. For reasons of space or time (e.g., in a journalistic report or article) or even for reasons of an author's viewpoint or emphases, it leaves things out. So John says at the end of his Gospel, "Jesus did many other things as well. If every one of them were written down, I suppose that even the whole world would not have room for the books that would be written" (John 21:25). John the historian left out a great deal that he could have written. He left some things out and thereby also allowed himself to be limited to communicating the things the Spirit wanted him

---

7. After the fall, the distinction applies to *humans* not in a personal covenantal relationship with Yahweh; so, e.g., it is Elohim, and not Yahweh, who speaks to Abimelech in a dream and warns him not to have Sarah in Gen 20. For this distinction between uses of the divine names "Elohim" and "Yahweh" in Genesis, see Umberto Cassuto, *The Documentary Hypothesis* (Jerusalem: Magnes, 1983), 18–49.

to communicate. Likewise, I here propose that the prior material
in Genesis 2 left out the datum that the Lord God prohibited even
touching the forbidden tree—and yet apparently, he did forbid it,
because one now has that information from the woman, who is not
yet in a state of sin and who does not report untrue things about
God. Her statement provides supplementary data not given in the
earlier account. That appears to be the way of Moses the historian
and, as will become apparent, of Luke the historian as well.

As was noted at the outset of this chapter, Genesis contains
two other historiographical examples relevant to the present study.
One example involves reported human speech; the other involves
reported divine speech.

A HUMAN EXAMPLE: GENESIS 12 AND 20

I have proposed that Adam's wife provided further data in Genesis 3
about the Lord God's command in Genesis 2. Another example
of a marriage partner giving more information about something
some time after it was first reported occurs in the matter of Abram/
Abraham and Sarai/Sarah with regard to Abimelech in Genesis 20.[8]

---

8. Readers will remember that Abraham's son, Isaac, tried the same ruse once,
on a subsequent Abimelech (perhaps a throne name) of Gerar:

"When the men of that place asked him about his wife, he said, 'She is my
sister,' because he was afraid to say, 'She is my wife.' He thought, 'The men
of this place might kill me on account of Rebekah, because she is beautiful.'
When Isaac had been there a long time, Abimelek king of the Philistines
looked down from a window and saw Isaac caressing his wife Rebekah. So
Abimelek summoned Isaac and said, 'She is really your wife! Why did you say,
"She is my sister?"' Isaac answered him, 'Because I thought I might lose my life
on account of her.' Then Abimelek said, 'What is this you have done to us?
One of the men might well have slept with your wife, and you would have
brought guilt upon us.' So Abimelek gave orders to all the people: 'Anyone
who harms this man or his wife shall surely be put to death.'" (Gen 26:7–11)

This is, apparently, a case of a son imitating his father—quite unwisely, as it turns
out. Some interpreters employ source criticism or argue for literary dependency to
explain the relationship of the two passages, but those alternatives seem unnecessary

Abram and Sarai go to Egypt. In the memorable account Abram tells his wife, "I know what a beautiful woman you are. When the Egyptians see you, they will say, 'This is his wife.' Then they will kill me but will let you live. Say you are my sister, so that I will be treated well for your sake and my life will be spared because of you" (Gen 12:11–13). Later, when Abraham and Sarah enter Gerar, Abraham plays the same trick. God (אלהים) warns Abimelech about Sarah in a dream. The king awakens and reproaches Abraham for his duplicity, which could have led to a grievous sin. Abraham explains:

> I said to myself, "There is surely no fear of God in this place, and they will kill me because of my wife." Besides, she really is my sister, the daughter of my father though not of my mother; and she became my wife. And when God had me wander from my father's household, I said to her, "*This is how you can show your love to me: Everywhere we go, say of me, 'He is my brother.'*" (Gen 20:11–13, emphasis added)

The information Abraham adds at this moment (i.e., the italicized v. 13b) would naturally surprise someone who has read his career from Genesis 12 onward. The historian reports how Abram played this trick in Genesis 12. The reader now knows he has played it again in Genesis 20. But only *now*, in Genesis 20, does one learn that Abraham had instructed his (half) sister to tell the same half-truth "everywhere we go."[9] Only now does one learn he told her, "This is how you can show your love to me."

---

since human nature would seem to account for Isaac's reported behavior well enough. For discussion and negative evaluation of literary-critical and source-critical attempts to understand the Abraham and Isaac accounts (although with a view of Scripture not shared in the present work), cf. T. D. Alexander, "Are the Wife/Sister Incidents of Genesis Literary Compositional Variants?," *VT* XLII.2 (1992): 145–53.

9. On Abraham's half-truth as a deception—and on deception more generally in the Old Testament, including deceptions by God himself—cf. *BT* 2, 281–310.

How many times did Abraham and Sarah (or Abram and Sarai) play this trick? There is no way to know. We do know this much: in Genesis 20:13b Abraham provides new and supplemental information about what he had told Sarai before. Here, then, is a clear case of laconic reporting by the historian who composed Genesis 12 (whom we affirm to be Moses in the case of both Genesis 2–3 and Genesis 12–20—and indeed of Genesis and the Pentateuch), now supplemented with additional information. The information is communicated by someone present earlier in the history (namely, Abraham) to someone later (namely, Abimelech), and conveniently it involves information regarding a man and his wife. What is apparently a historiographical fact in Genesis 20:13 as compared with Genesis 12:13 would seem to be a historiographical possibility with regard to Genesis 3:2–3 as compared with Genesis 2:16–17, especially since the historian is the same in both cases. The difference in the conditions (unfallen and fallen) of the players in these two dramas makes no historiographical difference, because the historian in both cases is the same. The compositional principle is also the same: a laconic third-person, "omniscient" report in the first instance supplemented by a later first-person report. Commentaries have not taken the historiographical implications of this aspect of the Genesis 20 narrative into account, as a review will show. Because the present case is ancillary to the discussion of Genesis 3:2–3 vis-à-vis Genesis 2:16–17, the sampling will be brief. Like the sampling related to Genesis 2 and 3, it will draw on Jewish, literary-critical, and evangelical scholarship.

MOSES BEN NAHMAN

Moses ben Nahman (AD 1194–1270), known as Nahmanides and also referred to by the acronym Ramban, was a leading Sephardic rabbi. Rabbi Meir Zlotowitz summarizes his commentary on the verse in question (Gen 20:13):

Ramban finds it difficult to see how this response [Abraham's explanation that Sarah was in fact his sister] met Abimelech's complaint; the critical factor in Abimelech's predicament was that she was also Abraham's wife. ... *Ramban* therefore maintains that Abraham's explanation of his motive was given in the previous and the next verse that this manner of identifying Sarah had been *routinely adopted* as a life-saving measure. The statement in this verse is merely an *additional justification* that he spoke the truth by declaring her his sister.[10]

Ramban essentially repeats what Abraham himself said: the patriarch adopted the ruse as "a life-saving measure." The rabbi seems comfortable with the fact that only now in the Abrahamic narrative does one learn this aspect of the history. Maybe, like most readers, he assumes or implicitly grants the historian's right to organize the material as seemed good to him—or, in the case of a divinely inspired history, as he was led to compose it.

GUNKEL, SKINNER, WESTERMANN, AND VAN SETERS

Scholars from a more liberal tradition do not show much concern about Genesis 12–22 as continuous historiography because they divide it into several sources and their main concern is to distinguish the sources. According to them, the Genesis 12 account is J and the Genesis 20 account is E. An account earlier than E naturally can be quite ignorant of material found in E.

---

10. Meir Zlotowitz, *Bereishis/Genesis: A New Translation with a Commentary from Talmudic, Midrashic and Rabbinic Sources* (Brooklyn: Mesorah Publications, 1977), 732–33. Emphases in Zlotowitz.

Hermann Gunkel

Hermann Gunkel sees the Genesis 12 and Genesis 20 accounts as the deposit of two different sources:

> The narrator has obviously invented ad hoc the detail, that Sarah was Abraham's half-sister; the old tradition of 11:29 knows nothing of that. —Marriages between half-siblings are not unheard of in ancient Israel II Sam 13:13, later not permitted Dtn 27:22, Lev 18:9.11, 20:17. —[V.] 13 is likewise supposed to be an excuse: Abraham has dealt so not only here, but always. The narrator—as it appears—has also concocted this ad hoc. The detail is actually a variant of [v.] 11; but one can well believe it of this rambling narrator, who, here, seeks as many excuses as possible.[11]

Genesis 11:29 does not mention the half-sibling aspect of Abraham and Sarah's relationship, but that only shows it is from an older source that did not know about it. The same would apply to the Genesis 12 account of Abram and Sarai because that material is from the earlier J source. The material in Genesis 20:13 is seen as an ad hoc excuse made up by a narrator who ranges far and wide for excuses that would exculpate Abraham.

---

11. Hermann Gunkel, *Genesis übersetzt und erklärt* (Göttingen: Vandenhoeck & Ruprecht, 1901), 202, author's translation. The German text reads: "Die Angabe, dass Sara Halbschwester Abrahams gewesen sei, hat der Erzähler augenscheinlich ad hoc erfunden; die alte Tradition 11:29 weiss nichts davon. — Ehen zwischen Halbgeschwistern sind im alten Israel nicht unerhört II Sam. 13:13, später unerlaubt Dtn. 27:22 Lev. 18:9.11 20:17. — 13 soll gleichfalls eine Entschuldigung sein: so hat Abraham nicht nur hier, sondern schon immer gehandelt. Auch dies hat der Erzähler — wie es scheint — ad hoc ersonnen. Eigentlich ist die Angabe eine Variante zu 11; ist aber diesem weitläufigen Erzähler, der hier nach möglichst vielen Entschuldigungsgründen sucht, wohl zuzutrauen." For Gunkel's source attributions see his discussion on the same page.

John Skinner

Skinner likewise attributes the Genesis 20 narrative to E:

> The chapter deals with an incident closely similar to that
> recorded in 12:10–20. It is indeed impossible to doubt that
> the two are variants of the same tradition. ... The narrative
> is the first continuous excerpt from E; and contains several
> stylistic and other peculiarities of that document. ... (18 יהוה
> is a gloss)... The appearing of God in a dream is character-
> istic of E; and the conception of Abraham as a prophet (7)
> is at least foreign to the original J.[12]

According to higher-critical tradition, J presents Yahweh anthropo-
morphically, but E presents God more remotely as one who communicates to prophets through dreams.[13] The presence of the name
"Yahweh" (v. 7) in this supposedly continuous E excerpt presents no
problem for such commentators, because it can be explained as a
gloss.[14]

Claus Westermann and J. van Seters

Claus Westermann follows a different approach, which sees the
Genesis 20 narrative not as a historical account but as a theological
reflection on the Genesis 12 story:

---

12. John Skinner, *A Critical and Exegetical Commentary on Genesis*, 2nd ed.
(Edinburgh: T&T Clark, 1994), 315.

13. Other scholars in the same tradition also attribute the Gen 12 account to J
and the Gen 20 account to E. See A. Dillmann, *Die Genesis*, 6th ed. (Leipzig: Hirzel,
1892), 226, 278–79, 322–23; E. König, *Die Genesis* (Gutersloh: Bertelsmann, 1925), 56–57,
67; E. A. Speiser, *Genesis* (Garden City, NY: Doubleday, 1964), 91; Gerhard von Rad,
Genesis: A Commentary, 2nd ed. (London: SCM, 1972), 226, 270.

14. Those familiar with literary criticism will recognize the characterization of
material that, according to the hermeneutic, does not suit the environment in which
it occurs, as a gloss, or an interpolation by another hand.

The story in Gen. 12:10–20 raised many questions for later times, particularly that of guilt, which gave rise to the subsequent rehearsal. ... It is more exegesis or reflection than narrative. ... When one compares Gen. 12 and 20 ... only 12:10–20 is a narrative about Abraham which has clearly arisen out of oral tradition. Gen. 20:1–18 is an adaptation which has grown out of reflection on a well-known narrative and shows all the characteristics of a literary origin.[15]

Westermann's view of the relationship of the Genesis 20 story to that of Genesis 12 resembles the view proposed earlier by J. van Seters. Van Seters believed that, unlike the Genesis 12 account, the Genesis 20 account, although it is a later treatment of the same story, has a different origin and motive: "It is another version of the same theme, which has the older account very much in mind and which seeks to answer certain important theological and moral issues that the narrator felt were inadequately treated in the earlier account."[16]

EXCURSUS:
BRIEF REFLECTIONS ON METHOD

It may be appropriate at this point to make some general observations about literary-critical, form-critical, oral-tradition, and traditio-historical hermeneutics since they have played and continue to play a major role in Old Testament interpretation, and such interpretations appear concerning the

---

15. Claus Westermann, *Genesis 12–36: A Commentary*, trans. John J. Scullion, SJ (Minneapolis: Fortress, 1985), 319; original ed. Claus Westermann, *Genesis 12–36*, Biblischer Kommentar, Altes Testament, I ii (Neukirchen-Vluyn: Neukirchener Verlag, 1981).

16. J. Van Seters, *Abraham in History and Tradition* (New Haven: Yale University Press, 1975), 173.

passages studied in this work. Comparative studies of the two Abrahamic passages (Gen 12, 20) in particular open the door to the following reflections.

The prevalence of the approaches just mentioned has produced a reaction on the part of some interpreters who, nonetheless, agree with these hermeneutics. One may think in particular of rhetorical criticism and, especially, canonical criticism. One who practices those approaches is able to do two things: (1) affirm the results of disjunctive analyses such as those of Gunkel, Skinner, Westermann, van Seters, and others, but also (2) interpret Genesis, the Pentateuch, the whole Old Testament, or the Bible as an integral whole. In other words, rhetorical and canonical criticism—perhaps especially, in recent history, the latter—make it possible to do biblical theology.[17] One might ask why the second point is true. The answer is quite simple: one cannot do a whole-biblical theology unless one treats the Bible as a whole. The same would apply to a biblical theology of a whole book of the Bible or to a biblical-theological treatment of two related passages, such as the one undertaken here. Traditional views of the Bible, whether held by Jewish, Catholic, Orthodox, or Protestant interpreters, have respected the Bible's many claims and indications that it offers true history (along with other

---

17. The major figure in canonical criticism (although he disliked the term) is, of course, Brevard Childs. See Brevard S. Childs, *Biblical Theology in Crisis* (Philadelphia: Westminster, 1970); Childs, *Biblical Theology of the Old and New Testaments: Theological Reflection on the Christian Bible* (Philadelphia: Fortress, 1993). For a prolific example of a rhetorical critic who presupposes the results of tradition-history, see Robert Polzin, *Moses and the Deuteronomist: A Literary Study of the Deuteronomistic History, Part 1* (Bloomington: Indiana University Press, 1993); Polzin, *Samuel and the Deuteronomist: A Literary Study of the Deuteronomistic History, Part 2* (Bloomington: Indiana University Press, 1993); Polzin, *David and the Deuteronomist: A Literary Study of the Deuteronomistic History, Part 3* (Bloomington: Indiana University Press, 1993).

genres, of course), including an accurate record of God's interventions and dealings with human beings. They have viewed the Bible as a true, coherent, and revealed/inspired whole. Those who do not hold that view of the Bible but who see, e.g., Genesis as an amalgam of various non-Mosaic sources in which oral tradition plays a role are left dealing with a variety that by hermeneutical definition lacks unity. Short of some new hermeneutical accommodation, such as rhetorical criticism or canonical criticism, the vast majority of Old Testament scholars from the eighteenth century to the present day have found it difficult to produce biblical theology and do not consider Genesis 12 and Genesis 20 as though they were both part of one coherent narrative stream that could be understood as a whole. Those hermeneutics would, moreover, prevent them from understanding Genesis 12 and Genesis 20 as continuous *historiography*. It also follows that the sorts of questions being explored in the present work do not arise as possible questions.

KEIL AND DELITZSCH, KIDNER, AND WENHAM

A brief sampling of evangelical scholarship completes the survey regarding the Genesis 12 and 20 accounts. None of these commentators would agree with the hermeneutics of source criticism, Gunkelian form criticism, or any approach that would create disjunction between the Genesis 12 and Genesis 20 accounts, but they do differ among themselves in some details.

Keil and Delitzsch

Nineteenth-century German scholars Keil and Delitzsch comment regarding Genesis 20:13 and Abraham in particular:

The latter had but two weak excuses: (1) that he supposed there was no fear of God at all in the land, and trembled for his life because of his wife; and (2) that when he left his father's house, he had arranged with his wife that in every foreign place she was to call herself his sister, as she really was his half-sister. On the subject of his emigration, he expressed himself indefinitely and with reserve, accommodating himself to the polytheistic standpoint of the Philistine king: "when God (or the gods, Elohim) caused me to wander," i.e., led me to commence an unsettled life in a foreign land; and saying nothing about Jehovah, and the object of his wandering as revealed by Him.[18]

Scholars before and after have noted the ambiguity of "Elohim." It is especially ambiguous in this case because Abraham uses it with a plural verb (התעו). That could be taken by Abimelech as "gods," which would suit a polytheistic understanding. Nonetheless Abimelech did experience a revelation from Elohim (Gen 20:6, "And Elohim spoke [sg. verb] to him in a dream," author's rendering; cf. 20:3), and the term "Elohim" does sometimes occur of the true God with a plural verb, as Driver noted.[19] Keil and Delitzsch say nothing about the relation of Abraham's second "weak excuse" (namely, that Abraham had asked Sarah to say she was his sister "everywhere" they went) to the earlier Abrahamic narrative sequence that omitted this detail (Gen 12:1–20:12).

---

18. C. F. Keil and F. Delitzsch, *Biblical Commentary on the Old Testament, Vol. 1., The Pentateuch*, trans. Rev. James Martin (Edinburgh: T&T Clark, 1885), 240.

19. Cf. S. R. Driver, *The Book of Genesis with Introduction and Notes* (London: Methuen & Co. Ltd., 1904), 250–51. See further comments below.

Derek Kidner

Derek Kidner likewise does not mention the possibility of prior laconic reporting regarding the data Abraham gives in Genesis 20:13, but he does offer a few broad moral reflections on Abraham's pattern of behavior, and he references the relevant verses of Genesis 20:

> Abraham's reply confessed to a pattern of mistaken choices which is in essence every man's with its fallibility in the realms of facts (11), values (the casuistry of 12) and motives (the cowardice of 13). The confession is marred by an attempt to shift the blame, Adam-like, in 13, which reads literally "… when (the) gods caused me to wander …" It is the language and very attitude of the pagan; one man of the world might be speaking to another.[20]

Scholarship has been divided as to the significance of Elohim coupled with a plural verb in verse 13. Suggestions range from relics of a less-strict use of the name Elohim, to a copyist's error, to what one finds when an Israelite speaks to a non-Israelite, to a plural of majesty (as at 2 Sam 7:23?), to an inclusion of God and angels (as at Gen 35:7 and possibly Exod 22:8 of God and his angelic judicial council, as clearly portrayed in 1 Kgs 22), to the triune nature of God.[21] What

---

20. Derek Kidner, *Genesis: An Introduction and Commentary* (Downers Grove, IL: InterVarsity Press, 1967), 138–39.

21. For the less strict use or the copyist's error suggestion, cf. C. J. Ellicott, *A Bible Commentary for English Readers*, vol. 1 (London: Cassell, 1905); for an Israelite speaking to a non-Israelite, cf. Herbert E. Ryle, *The Book of Genesis*, *The Cambridge Bible for Schools and Colleges*, ed. A. F. Kirkpatrick (Cambridge: University Press, 1914), and also Keil; for plural of majesty, cf. Thomas Whitelaw, *Genesis*, in *The Pulpit Commentary, Vol. 1* (Grand Rapids: Eerdmans, 1950); for angels or inclusion of angels, cf. John Calvin, *Commentaries on the First Book of Moses Called Genesis, Volume First*, trans. Rev. John King (Grand Rapids: Eerdmans, 1948); for the triune God, cf. John Gill, *Exposition of the Bible*, https://www.biblestudytools.com/commentaries/gills -exposition-of-the-bible/genesis-20-13.html. Regarding verse 13, Calvin in his commentary simply remarks, "Sarah, by agreement, had always said the same thing which she had done in Gerar" (Calvin, *Genesis*, 431). Gordon Wenham, *Genesis 16–50*,

matters more for the present study is the supplemental information Abraham provides when he makes his excuse.

Gordon Wenham

Gordon Wenham rejects the views developed by Westermann and earlier higher critics and takes the Genesis 20 account as history. He introduces a novel possibility regarding verse 13, however:

> The rest of Abraham's excuse is also weak. It is especially remarkable that he claims that his behavior in Gerar was his general policy: "wherever we go, say for me, 'He is my brother,'" for back in 12:12 (presupposed here) this is presented as a device used once only in Egypt. Certainly the intervening episodes never give a hint that Abraham used this story after his expulsion from Egypt. So what are we to make of this discrepancy? Since there is much evidence that the writer of chap. 20 was fully conversant with the preceding material in Genesis ... we cannot simply explain this as E's view as opposed to J's. Rather, we conclude that either Abraham was not being quite truthful in saying this was his usual policy, when he had in fact only once before pretended Sarah was merely his sister, or that he was telling the truth and that wherever he went he misled people about Sarah's marital status. Neither explanation redounds to Abraham's credit. The first view seems the more likely. But both interpretations make him less of a saint than might be concluded from other passages.[22]

WBC 2 (Waco, TX: Word, 1994), notes: "It is unusual that 'God' here takes the plural verb, suggesting that 'gods' might be a better translation, and this may represent an accommodation to Abimelech's polytheistic outlook. But the majority of commentators see the plural verb as an anomaly" (73). Cf. E. Kautsch and A. E. Cowley, eds., *Gesenius' Hebrew Grammar* (Oxford: Clarendon, 1910), 145.

22. Gordon Wenham, *Genesis 16–50*, WBC 2 (Waco, TX: Word, 1994), 73.

Did Abraham mislead only Pharaoh and Abimelech, or did he also mislead (or intend to mislead) others as he, in effect, claimed? Wenham is right to say, "Neither explanation redounds to Abraham's credit." This important question may seem irresolvable. Either Abraham told Abimelech the truth, or he did not. If not, one could say Abraham, caught in a trick, was desperate to exonerate himself any way he could. Such a falsehood could bring to mind two possibilities:

1. Generalizing his deception could perhaps lessen it in Abimelech's eyes: after all, Abimelech may have been badly used, but he was not the only victim!

2. On the other hand, generalizing it could make it look even worse: Abraham was such a scoundrel he would do this to anyone and everyone.

One might argue that Abraham, a man of faith, would not now lie to Abimelech about his prior use of the same trick. But it seems doubtful one can make a case for Abraham's honesty about this fact on the basis of Abraham's overall condition of faith—not even on the evidence of his attested faith in Genesis 15, his unwavering faith regarding the promise of a child (cf. Rom 4:20), or his obedience in Genesis 22 (cf. Heb 11:8–12). Abraham cannot be a character witness in his own defense because someone who is faithful and good even with impressive consistency can still be weak in one area, even repeatedly so. Another argument for Abraham's honesty in this matter (i.e., his testimony in Gen 20:13) is possible, however—one that depends not on Abraham's faith credentials but on the immediate circumstance in which he finds himself. The argument, and the view taken here, is that Abraham, when his trick had just been exposed by God, would not be likely to add another sin to his fault and lie about his past behavior. His testimony to Abimelech is more likely to be true. On that basis his statement in Genesis 20:13 as compared with Genesis 12:12–13 would be another example of the sort of historiography I have sought to demonstrate: a third-person omniscient account, supplemented with more information afterward by a first-person account. Even if one doubts Abraham on this matter, however, the next example places the issue beyond doubt, for the one who supplements the prior history in that case is the Lord himself, and he is no liar.

A DIVINE EXAMPLE: ABRAHAMIC COVENANT NARRATIVES AND GENESIS 26:5

The most persuasive example of the historiographical phenomenon under consideration may be a case in which God himself is reported as saying more than he was first reported to have said. When the Lord reaffirms the Abrahamic covenant with Isaac he says: "Abraham obeyed My voice and kept My charge, My commandments, My statutes, and My laws" (Gen 26:5 NKJV).[23] The terms used ("obeyed my voice," "charge," "commandments," "statutes," and "laws") are used later of the Lord's requirements under the Mosaic covenant, but nowhere in the Abrahamic covenant-related material (broadly, Gen 12–22) are these terms used of any commands the Lord gave to Abraham with the single exception of "obeyed my voice" (the idiom, שמע בקול, Gen 22:18).[24] The Lord here is himself

---

23. For the Lord's reaffirmation of the Abrahamic covenant with Isaac, and subsequently with Jacob, as a reaffirmation and not a formal covenant renewal, see Niehaus, *BT* 2, 110.

24. In fact Gen 26:5 contains the first occurrences of "charge" [משמרת], "commandments" [מצות], "statutes" [חקות], and "laws" [תורת] in the Bible. The Lord does say, "For I have known him, in order that he may command his children and his household after him, that they keep the way of the LORD, to do righteousness and justice, that the LORD may bring to Abraham what He has spoken to him" (Gen 18:19 NKJV), but this both alludes to possible prior unreported torah and also falls short

adding information—and information, one should note, about his own commands—not provided by the historian in the earlier, laconic Abrahamic narratives.

RASHI AND RAMBAN

Ramban, cited above, believes that Abraham received the entire Mosaic law before it was given, and he cites Rashi to that effect:

> *Ramban* cites Rashi's interpretation which implies that Abraham fulfilled the Torah before it was revealed at Sinai. Indeed this is the opinion of the sages. ... *Ramban* explains that the consensus of Rabbinic opinion is that Abraham arrived at a knowledge of the *entire Torah* through Divine inspiration and observed it voluntarily. ... Before the Torah was given, however, the Patriarchs observed the future commandments without exception only in *Eretz Israel.*[25]

Ironically the ancient Jewish interpreters see in Genesis 26:5 an indication that Abraham possessed the whole Mosaic law, a conclusion not much different from the critical scholars' view that the verse represents a retrojection from the later pentateuchal materials. The crucial difference, of course, is that the older Jewish interpreters did not see Genesis 26:5 as evidence of a later "Deuteronomic hand" but as evidence of prior revelation by God to Abraham.[26]

---

of the terminological specificity one finds in Gen 26:5. For a discussion of the verb "to know" in relation to divine election, see Niehaus, *BT* 3, 113–16.

25. Zlotowitz, *Bereishis*, 1083–84. For discussion of Gen 26:5 generally and of the particular terms and how Jewish interpretive tradition understood them in relation to the patriarch and the Mosaic law, see Zlotowitz, *Bereishis*, 1082–85.

26. One could see a key phrase in Gen 18:19 as consonant with this view: "For I have chosen him, so that he will direct his children and his household after him to keep the way of the LORD by doing *what is right and just*, so that the LORD will bring about for Abraham what he has promised him." The pair "right and just" (NIV, emphasis added; lit. "righteousness and justice," צדקה ומשפט, cf. NKJV), occurs as characteristic of the Lord himself (e.g., Pss 89:14; 97:2; cf. Deut 32:4; 33:21) and of

DRIVER, RYLE, AND WESTERMANN

Critical scholars generally think the passage is Deuteronomic or largely Deuteronomic. The separation of Deuteronomy from the first four books of the Pentateuch traces back to W. M. L. de Wette, who first proposed it in a thesis. It subsequently became a governing concept in liberal Old Testament scholarship and remains so to the present day.[27]

S. R. Driver

S. R. Driver follows in this tradition. He displays the subsequent use of the terms found in Genesis 26:5, chiefly in Deuteronomy and Leviticus, but does not credit them to the time of Isaac:

> No such expressions are used elsewhere in connexion with the patriarchs. The obedience of Abraham is described here in terms borrowed from the Mosaic law; thus, for "charge," see Lev. xviii. 20, xxii. 9, Dt. xi, 1; for "commandments" and "statutes," Dt. vi. 2, xxviii. 45, xxx. 10; and for "laws," Lev. xxvi. 46, Ex. xliv, 23.[28]

Even if one thought the author who borrowed these terms from the Mosaic law was Moses himself (which Driver does not suppose), it would not help the historicity of the account because it would have Moses putting words into God's mouth as part of his narrative art.

---

obedience to his law (cf. Isa 1:21; 5:7; Jer 22:15; Ezek 45:9) and of the future messianic king/Lord who will fulfill that law (cf. Isa 9:7, 16:5; Hos 2:9).

27. Cf. W. M. L. de Wette, *Dissertatio Critica qua Deuteronomium diversum a prioribus Pentateuchi libris, alius cuiusdam recentioris autoris opus esse demonstratur* (Jena 1805). For an online translation into English, see https://scholarsphere.psu.edu/downloads/djh343s422.

28. S. R. Driver, *The Book of Genesis*, 250–51.

Herbert E. Ryle

Herbert E. Ryle similarly notes that the sequence of "my charge ... my laws" does not fit the days of Isaac:

> A strange redundancy of expression, reminding us of the style of Deut. The four words "charge," "commandments," "statutes," "laws," correspond to the more simple phrase "the way of the Lord" in 18:19. The observance of legal enactments, ascribed to Abraham, is, strictly speaking, an anachronism. Cf. Deut. 11:1, "Therefore thou shall love the Lord thy God, and keep his charge, and his statutes, and his judgments, and his commandments, alway."[29]

Of course, the fact that the terms in question were used later to describe "legal enactments" that were part of the Mosaic covenant does not prove they are anachronisms in an account regarding Abraham. Crediting the historicity of the account, the present work accepts that, according to Genesis 26:5, the Lord had given Abraham these requirements and he had obeyed them. Additionally, it seems reasonable to suppose that the same "charge," "commandments," "statutes," and "laws" showed up later in the Mosaic law *along with many others* (just as the death penalty for murder in the Noahic covenant showed up later in the Mosaic covenant *along with the death penalty for other acts*, e.g., blasphemy, adultery), but one cannot prove this.

Claus Westermann

Because of the Deuteronomic flavor of the phrases, Westermann puts the passage even later:

---

29. Herbert E. Ryle, *The Book of Genesis*, *The Cambridge Bible for Schools and Colleges*, ed. A. F. Kirkpatrick (Cambridge: University Press, 1914), 274.

> But Abraham is here the exemplar of obedience to the law
> in return for which God bestowed the promises on him;
> this can have been pronounced and written only in a period
> when Israel's relationship to God was centered on its obe-
> dience to the law; that would be the post-Deuteronomic
> period, as the language of v. 5 clearly shows.[30]

As has been argued, this way of construing the material is actually
backward, unless one views the Lord's words to Isaac as a fabrica-
tion. Nonetheless, some evangelical scholars have thought the same
way (see below). In any case, this tradition of interpretation never
takes up the possibility that the Lord is providing, in Genesis 26:5,
supplementary information not given in the earlier Abrahamic
narratives (Gen 12–22) because the hermeneutic it employs rules
out that possibility.

KEIL AND DELITZSCH, WALTKE, AND WENHAM

Evangelical scholars generally pass over the additional information in Genesis 26:5 without much discussion of its historiographical aspect vis-à-vis Genesis 12–22. It seems to be taken for granted
that the Lord did, indeed, make this statement to Isaac, but no
comparison is made with other biblical cases, or possible cases, of
a third-person omniscient account supplemented later by a first-
person account of the same words or events.

Keil and Delitzsch

Keil and Delitzsch offer a brief comment but do not reflect on its
implications for or relationship to the earlier Abrahamic material:

---

30. Westermann, *Genesis 12–36*, 424–25.

The piety of Abraham is described in words that indicate a perfect obedience to all the commands of God, and therefore frequently recur among the legal expressions of a later date. שָׁמַר מִשְׁמֶרֶת יְהוָה "to take care of Jehovah's care," i.e., to observe Jehovah, His person, and His will, *Mishmereth*, reverence, observance, care, is more closely defined by "*commandments, statutes, laws*," to denote constant obedience to all the revelations and instructions of God.[31]

Apart from noting that "commandments, statutes, laws" more closely define "charge" (the usual translation of משמרת, e.g., ASV, ESV, NKJV, NASB; "everything I required of him," NIV; "mandate," CSB), the commentary does not explore how the provision of the additional data may implicate a broader pattern of historiographical narrative art. In particular, Keil and Delitzsch do not explore the relationship of Genesis 26:5 to the earlier Abrahamic narrative material (Gen 12–22).

Bruce Waltke

Bruce Waltke, by contrast, offers what may seem an ambiguous understanding of Genesis 26:5: it can be a reference either to some teaching given to "the patriarchs" or to the whole law revealed later to Moses.

The many synonyms for *law* connote Abraham's comprehensive obedience to God's rule over him. The narrator means either the teaching of piety and ethics known by the patriarchs prior to Moses or more probably the whole law of Moses. Genesis is part of the Pentateuch and should be interpreted in that context. In Deut. 11:1 the same list of

---

31. C. F. Keil and F. Delitzsch, *Biblical Commentary on the Old Testament, Vol. 1., The Pentateuch*, trans. Rev. James Martin (Edinburgh: T&T Clark, 1885), 270.

terms refers to the whole law of Moses. The text shows that
the person of faith does not live by law but keeps the law
(see Gen. 15:6, 22:1–19; Heb. 11:8–19).[32]

Waltke's last comment is true in principle, but it is not what the
text says: the text of Genesis 26 does *not* indicate that the person of
faith does not live by the law. It does indicate that the person of faith
(Abraham, in this case) *keeps* the law(s) of whatever covenant(s) he
is under. In Abraham's case, that would mean the Adamic, Noahic,
and Abrahamic covenants to the extent that those "laws" still
applied (e.g., Abraham was fruitful and multiplied, by the Lord's
enabling, but some other laws of the Adamic covenant could not
apply—Abraham was not under any law regarding the tree of life,
etc.). So, with regard to the Abrahamic covenant and any requirements the Lord gave him in that covenant, "Abraham obeyed My
voice and kept My charge, My commandments, My statutes, and
My laws," Gen 26:5 NKJV). The text tells nothing more than that. In
Abraham's case he kept requirements that would (probably) become
part of the later Mosaic law, but there is no proof that he had the
whole Mosaic law.

The substance of Waltke's analysis, unfortunately, does not
bear up under scrutiny: "The narrator means either the teaching
of piety and ethics known by the patriarchs prior to Moses or more
probably the whole law of Moses." If the Lord refers to standards
he gave Abraham before—standards presumably passed on from
Abraham to Isaac and Jacob ("teaching of piety and ethics known
by the patriarchs prior to Moses"), then we may have here another

---

32. Bruce K. Waltke and Cathi J. Fredricks, *Genesis: A Commentary* (Grand Rapids:
Zondervan, 2001), 368. Note however that Deut 11:1 omits "my laws" (תורת, Gen 26:5).
Cf. somewhat similarly Kidner, *Genesis*, 153: "The heaped-up terms (*cf., e.g.,* Dt. 11:1)
suggest the complete servant, responsible and biddable. They also dispel any idea
that law and promise are in necessary conflict (*cf.* Jas. 2:22; Gal. 3:12)."

case of laconic reporting (in Gen 12–22), supplemented by further information (in Gen 26:5). If, however, we suppose that the Lord refers to the *whole* Mosaic law ("more probably the whole law of Moses"), there is unfortunately no evidence that Abraham had the whole law.[33] But to be clear: Waltke does not say or even suggest the Lord had actually given Abraham the whole law some time before. Rather, he reckons Abraham's possession of the whole law may be assumed *as part of the narrative* ("the narrator intends") in Genesis 26:5. This is so because "Genesis is part of the Pentateuch and should be interpreted in that context." Many would agree with that statement. But it does imply a question: What does it look like if Genesis is interpreted in the context of the Pentateuch? It could mean—as it is here affirmed—that (in the case of Genesis 26:5) we are told the Lord gave Abraham a certain "charge" and certain "commandments," "statutes," and "laws" that also appeared later, along with many others, in the Mosaic covenant. There is no necessity—beyond mere terminological resemblance—that one think later ideas were imported into Genesis 26:5 just because both Genesis 26:5 and the later Mosaic torah are part of the Pentateuch.

This line of reasoning also entails a moral problem. It effectively makes the historian, Moses, a liar: Moses puts into the Lord's mouth a claim that Abraham had something he did not in fact have, "the whole law." Presumably, from this point of view, the falsehood of the claim would not matter to a later reader, since the later reader would read Genesis 26:5 with Deuteronomy, for example, in mind. Alternatively, one might infer the meaning (for Gen 26:5) that Abraham kept the whole Mosaic law, even though he did not actually have it—but that is, apparently, not what Waltke suggests. Unfortunately, this approach to the material gives the Lord's words to Abraham a meaning no one can demonstrate those words

---

33. Recall, however, that some of the older Jewish interpreters held the same view.

possess.[34] A simpler and more natural explanation would not read the whole Mosaic law back into Genesis 26:5. Rather it affirms that the Lord had given Abraham some charge, commandments, statutes, and laws that he also gave later, with many more added, in the Sinai covenant and its renewal, Deuteronomy.

Gordon Wenham

Gordon Wenham offers a less speculative way of looking at the material. In the course of doing so he also disputes the backward reading that has been a standard for critical scholars:

> This verse expands 22:18b, "because you have obeyed me." The addition, "kept my instructions, commandments, statutes, and my laws," reinforce and underline the extent and thoroughness of Abraham's obedience. Though often said to be a typically Deuteronomic phase, in fact, "keep my instruction" occurs only once in Deuteronomy (Deut 11:1) but much more frequently in priestly texts in Leviticus and Numbers. Similarly, "keep my commandments," "keep my statutes," and "keep my laws" are frequent phrases in priestly texts but less typical of Deuteronomy, which never speaks of laws in the plural. Presumably, this text has been ascribed to deuteronomistic editing because it strings together terms, but this is more a feature of rhetorical style than authorship.[35]

Unquestionably, the verse expands on Genesis 22:18b, and it certainly does "reinforce and underline the extent and thoroughness of Abraham's obedience." In fact it expands upon—or, to use a term consonant with the present study, supplements—the whole body

---

34. Unless Waltke has been remarkably unclear and does not mean what his words seem to mean. Taken as we take them, at least, they have some family resemblance to Townsend's later approach to the early Genesis narratives (cf. chapter 3).

35. Wenham, *Genesis 16–50*, 190.

of material that documents the Lord's dealing with Abraham from Genesis 12 though Genesis 22.

OVERALL CONCLUSION
REGARDING GENESIS DATA

If one considers the ways interpreters have compared the passages (Gen 12:13 // Gen 20:13; Gen 12–22 // Gen 26:5)—the methods they have employed and the conclusions they have reached—several things stand out from the history of interpretation. The following display summarizes the major views of the earlier Jewish interpreters and of the critical and evangelical interpreters surveyed above.

REGARDING GENESIS 12:13 // GENESIS 20:13

1. Ramban essentially repeats what Abraham himself said: the patriarch adopted the ruse as "a life-saving measure." The rabbi seems comfortable with the supplemental data. He implicitly grants the historian's right to organize his material as seems good to him.

2. Critical scholars see the two passages as variants of the same tradition, either documentary (e.g., Skinner) or oral (Gunkel). Westermann takes a different approach and sees the later passage as a literary-theological reflection on an earlier account that has an oral provenance.

3. Scholars in the evangelical tradition take the texts at face value (Keil and Delitzsch), seeing Abraham's excuses to Abimelech as "a pattern of mistaken choices which is in essence every man's with its fallibility" (Kidner), although Wenham offers a different and intriguing ambiguity: Abraham either gave

us supplemental information when he explained his previously used trick to Abimelech or he lied to Abimelech when he said he had told Sarah to practice this trick wherever they went. This novel proposal could be correct, though I think it unlikely that Abraham would lie again just after being exposed by God as a liar or, at best, a teller of a half truth.

REGARDING GENESIS 12–22 // GENESIS 26:5

1. The ancient Jewish interpreters see in Genesis 26:5 an indication that Abraham possessed the whole Mosaic law, although we only learn this in Genesis 26:5.

2. Scholars in the critical tradition tend to see the statement of Genesis 26:5 as Deuteronomic (e.g., Driver, Ryle), although Westermann sees it as post-Deuteronomic.

3. Scholars in the evangelical tradition usually take Genesis 26:5 at face value and think the Lord provides new information (e.g., Keil and Delitzsch), although Waltke is ambiguous on the matter and thinks the narrator means either the teaching of piety and ethics known by the patriarchs prior to Moses or, more probably, the whole law of Moses. On that view the verse does not give the Lord's words but the words a narrator attributes to him, and the narrator probably has the whole law of Moses in mind. There is unfortunately no proof for this idea; it does rely on phraseological resemblance between the statement in Genesis 26 and a similar concatenation of terms in Deuteronomy 11.

Although it superficially resembles the older Jewish view that Abraham had the whole law, it is closer in spirit to critical scholarship that thinks the material is a Deuteronomic retrojection. Finally, Wenham rejects the backward reading of critical scholars. He explains that Genesis 26:5 expands on Genesis 22:18b and actually underlines the extent and thoroughness of Abraham's obedience.

The present work agrees with Wenham and the mainstream evangelical tradition as regards Genesis 26:5. The verse expands upon—or, I would say, supplements—the whole body of material that documents the Lord's dealing with Abraham from Genesis 12 though Genesis 22. Implicit in this view, held by Wenham and other evangelical scholars, is the concept of laconic reporting by Moses, although interpreters do not use the term "laconic" or explore it as a feature of biblical historiography beyond the instance at hand. The same is true of evangelical commentaries on Genesis 20:13 as compared with Genesis 12:13. There has been no comparison of the cases as historiography or discussion of their possible relevance to a historiographical understanding of Genesis 3:3b vis-à-vis Genesis 2:17b.

When viewed together, however, these three biblical cases appear to have one important thing in common. They are all examples of earlier, apparently laconic, third-person omniscient reporting (composed by the historian) supplemented by later first-person accounts of those earlier events (also composed by the historian). With regard to these cases, one might question the woman's accuracy of recall in Genesis 3:3 or Abraham's honesty in Genesis 20:13, but one cannot question God's accuracy of recall or honesty in Genesis 26:5, where the Lord himself is the one who provides the additional information. Moreover, earlier discussion has indicated the problematic nature of the proposal that a sinless human being (namely, Adam or his wife before the fall) could have been created with a faulty memory—a condition that would inevitably lead to sin and indeed would be sin in the realm of thought (by not amening God)—or that Abraham would lie again just after being caught in a lie (or a half truth) and exposed by God.

I have proposed that, with regard to the issue at hand, the most likely understanding of the two cases in Genesis just considered is that they offer parallel examples of laconic reporting supplemented by an individual's account given some time later. All three cases considered thus far occur in Genesis and were composed by the same inspired author, Moses. Luke appears to have used a kindred historiographical technique with regard to Paul's Damascus road experience in Acts.

5

LUKE AND PAUL

It may be good at this stage to restate the formal issue under consideration before moving on to a study of the accounts of Paul's Damascus road experience in Acts. The issue is purely one of historiography (although it can have theological implications or imply theological questions).[1] Posed as an abstract and formal issue: Does the Old Testament, and in particular Genesis, present a historiographical sequence of the following sort?

1. A third-person "omniscient" narrative of an event, followed by

2. a first-person recounting of the same event, adding more information about the event,

3. both composed as part of a narrative sequence by the same historian.

The primary instance, the third-person omniscient account presented in Genesis 2:17b by the historian, Moses, alongside the

---

1. As was noted and discussed to some extent in chapter 1 and will be discussed further at the end of the present work.

first-person account provided by the woman in Genesis 3:3b, also presented by Moses, has been the driving case for the present work. I have reviewed some of the commentary on those verses and have found that virtually none of the commentaries consulted have thought the woman was simply adding information that had not been provided in the earlier, laconic account.

I have proposed that subsequent cases of the same historiographical technique in Genesis should be located, if possible, and evaluated, to see if they could provide something like corroborating or supporting evidence for the proposed understanding of the relation between Genesis 2:17b and Genesis 3:17b. This has been shown to be especially worth doing since none of the scholars who commented on the verses in Genesis 2 and 3 appear to have explored the question of whether subsequent comparable historiographical cases might be found, even in Genesis, and if so, what bearing such facts might have on the right understanding of the reports in Genesis 2 and 3.

Two very noteworthy cases of that sort do exist, however, and we have located and discussed them and reviewed some of their attendant scholarship. We have compared the accounts in Genesis 12:13 and 20:13 and then the Abrahamic material in Genesis 12–22 vis-à-vis the Lord's summary statement in Genesis 26:5. We concluded that the most likely understanding of the two later cases in Genesis was that they offer parallel examples of laconic, third-person omniscient reporting supplemented by a first-person account given subsequently. All three cases considered so far occur in Genesis and come from the same inspired author, Moses.

Another, more detailed example of historiographical contrasts appears in the New Testament: the set of reports comprising Luke's account of Paul's Damascus road experience in Acts 9, and Paul's later recounting of the same experience in Acts 22, before the crowd in Jerusalem, and in Acts 26, before Festus and Agrippa. As a matter of historiography, a comparison of the three accounts of Paul's Damascus road experience—if the set they constitute proves to be comparable to what has been seen so far—could further commend the proposed understanding regarding the two accounts of the Lord's command about the tree in Genesis 2 and 3.[2] It has been argued (quite possibly mistakenly, as I have proposed) that the woman can be faulted for changing what God said at several points when she recounts, in Genesis 3, the command and permission of Genesis 2. At this final stage of our study of that issue, the Acts data may offer a useful historiographical parallel.[3]

It should be noted that not all scholars think the accounts in Acts report historical data. The present study considers the reports to be accurate historiography and will not explore more skeptical scholarship, but one example may serve to illustrate it. Hans Conzelmann comments on the Acts 9 account:

> There are two more accounts of Paul's call, in 22:1–26 and 26:9–18. The three versions are generally in agreement, but there are differences and even contradictions in details.

---

2. Scholars have sometimes compared Paul's theophanic encounter on the Damascus road with experiences of some Old Testament prophets and considered the relationship between conversion and call. So C. K. Barrett, *A Critical and Exegetical Commentary on the Acts of the Apostles, Volume I*, International Critical Commentary (Edinburgh: T&T Clark, 1994), 442, notes: "Of greater importance [than the parallels between Acts 9, 22 and 26] as parallels are the Old Testament stories of the call of prophets, notably Isa 6.1–13; Jer 1.4–10; cf. Gal 1.15. These parallels suggest the question, raised acutely by K. Stendahl ... whether the event should be described as a conversion or a call. The fact is that it is both: a conversion in the Christian sense is always at the same time a call." Barrett does go on however to distinguish usefully between conversion and vocation. For the Stendahl reference, cf. K. Stendahl, *Paul among Jews and Gentiles and Other Essays* (London: SCM Press, 1977), 7–23.

3. Many scholars note some of the differences between the accounts in Acts 9 and Acts 22 without particularly outlining them, and agree there is no contradiction between the accounts, although they assume Paul modifies his account in Acts 22 in order better to address his Jewish audience. Cf. Darrell. L. Bock, *Acts* (Grand Rapids: Baker Academic, 2007), 660–61; Craig S. Keener, *Acts: An Exegetical Commentary* (Grand Rapids: Baker Academic, 2013), 3195–99, 3227–32.

Does this mean that Luke used various sources? No. The repetition is for stylistic reasons, and the differences can be explained as literary variations (and, in part, as carelessness); they are linked with the adaptation of the material for the particular situation. The source is not an autobiographical account of an experience (for this reason a psychological explanation is wrongheaded), but a legend, with typical features.[4]

The "typical features" of legend include the appearance of light, a falling down, and a limitation of the appearance to the one for whom the vision is intended. Most scholars would probably now agree with Conzelmann's rejection of a source-critical approach to the three accounts.[5] His dismissal of the historical evidence may be too casual and unsupported, however, and the validity of any "legendary" characterization of the history cannot be proven beyond a reasonable doubt in the New Testament any more than it can in the Old Testament (e.g., in Genesis, where the category has been most often employed, especially since Gunkel's work on Genesis).[6]

Before considering the Lukan data, it would be appropriate to revisit the point made in the foreword to this work. Considerations of how Moses' or Luke's contemporaries wrote history or biography do not address the most important aspects of historiography

---

4. Hans Conzelmann, *Acts of the Apostles*, trans. James Limburg, A. Thomas Kraabel, and Donald H. Juel (Philadelphia: Fortress, 1987), 72.

5. For proposed source analysis, see Emanuel Hirsch, "Die Drei Berichte der Apostelgeschichte über die Bekehrung des Paulus," *ZNW* 28 (1929): 305–12. As Barrett, *A Critical and Exegetical Commentary*, 444, notes: "The view is now very generally abandoned that [Luke] used three distinct sources in Acts 9, 22, 26. The three accounts differ not because they reached Luke by different channels but in accordance with the contexts in which they are placed." More will be said below about the reports and their contexts.

6. Cf. Hermann Gunkel, *Genesis übersetzt und erklärt* (Göttingen: Vandenhoeck & Ruprecht, 1901).

in either the Old Testament or the New. Those aspects are, especially, (1) the divine-human covenant-centered nature of biblical history and historiography and (2) the reality of divine providence and intervention in shaping both. So much are these the essence of the matter that I have elsewhere characterized biblical history and historiography, and therewith the Bible itself, as the "annals of the Great King."[7]

As for the divine providence and intervention that shaped biblical history, together they constitute the most glaring difference between biblical and ancient Near Eastern historiography. The Bible records God's active and most importantly his miraculous intervention to a degree absolutely unparalleled in the ancient world. In the New Testament, Paul's Damascus road experience is an outstanding example of such intervention.

ACTS 9 AND 22

Luke's account of Paul's Damascus road experience and Paul's later accounts of the same before the Jews in Jerusalem and then before Festus and Agrippa, when taken together, illustrate additions and clarifications similar to those noted between Genesis 2:17 and Genesis 3:1–3. The following simple outline may illustrate the point:

1   In Genesis 2 the historian Moses records what the Lord God said to Adam regarding the trees.

2   In Genesis 3 the woman recounts to an audience (the serpent) what God said.

1′   In Acts 9 the historian Luke records what the Lord said to Paul and what followed.

---

7. Cf. *BT* 1, 3–6; *BT* 2, 278; *BT* 3, 343, 345.

2′   In Acts 22 Paul recounts to an audience (the Jews) what the Lord said and what followed.

2″   In Acts 26 Paul recounts to an audience (Festus and Agrippa) what the Lord said and what followed.

Ross and Beale have found points of difference between the historian's account in Genesis 2 and the woman's recounting in Genesis 3, and for them the differences point to error and/or self-will on the part of the woman. However, similar types of differences occur between the historian's account in Acts 9 and Paul's recountings in Acts 22 and 26. The following narrative display introduces the points of difference between Luke's account and Paul's recounting in Jerusalem. The Acts 9 and 22 data are displayed and discussed first and then Paul's account in Acts 26. The most notable differences in Acts 22 and 26 from Luke's Acts 9 account are in italics.

Acts 9:3–8

As he neared Damascus on his journey, suddenly a light from heaven flashed around him. He fell to the ground and heard a voice say to him, "Saul, Saul, why do you persecute me?"

"Who are you, Lord?" Saul asked.

"I am Jesus, whom you are persecuting," he replied. "Now get up and go into the city, and you will be told what you must do."

The men traveling with Saul stood there speechless; they heard the sound but did not see anyone. Saul got up from the ground, but when he opened his eyes he could see nothing. So they led him by the hand into Damascus. For three days he was blind, and did not eat or drink anything.

Acts 22:6–11

"*About noon* as I came near Damascus, suddenly a *bright light* from heaven flashed around me. I fell to the ground and heard a voice say to me, 'Saul! Saul! Why do you persecute me?'

"'Who are you, Lord?' I asked.

"'I am Jesus *of Nazareth*, whom you are persecuting,' he replied. *My companions saw the light, but they did not understand the voice of him who was speaking to me.*

"'What shall I do, Lord?' I asked.

"'Get up,' the Lord said, 'and go into *Damascus*. There you will be told *all that* you *have been assigned to do*.' *My companions* led me by the hand into Damascus, *because the brilliance of the light had blinded me.*"

Paul adds to or clarifies the earlier report in the following ways:[8]

Acts 9 Luke's account	Acts 22 Paul's recounting
[3] As	[6] About noon
[3] a light from heaven flashed around him	[6] a bright light from heaven flashed around me
[5] "Jesus"	[8] "Jesus of Nazareth"
	[10] "What shall I do, Lord?" I asked.
[6] "go into the city"	[10] "go into Damascus"

---

8. Eckhard Schnabel, *Acts,* Zondervan Exegetical Commentary on the New Testament (Grand Rapids: Zondervan, 2012), 902, has appreciated the differences between the Acts 9 account and the Acts 22 account in much the same way as we are about to do: "Many of the differences that distinguish Paul's account here with Luke's account in 9:1–19 can be explained by the fact that Paul describes events as they unfolded for him, while the earlier account is given by an 'omniscient' narrator."

⁶ "what you must do"	¹⁰ "all that you have been assigned to do"
⁷ they heard the sound but did not see anyone	⁹ My companions saw the light but did not understand the voice of him who was speaking to me.
⁸ when he opened his eyes he could see nothing	¹¹ the brilliance of the light had blinded me
⁸ So they led	¹¹ My companions led

Paul makes what appear to be nine changes, but they could just as well be characterized as additions or clarifications to the Acts 9 account. Sometimes he apparently adds information: it happened at *noon*, the light was *bright*, *the brilliance* of the light had blinded him.[9] Or he paraphrases or explicates what happened: it was his companions who led him into Damascus. But a couple of times he reports *other words from the mouth of the Lord* than were reported in Acts 9: the Lord said "I am Jesus of *Nazareth*" (an addition possibly to clarify which Jesus this was, for his present Jewish audience, although it is possible Jesus identified himself in this way during the theophany itself in Acts 9, and Luke did not record it there); the Lord will show "*all that* you *have been assigned to do*" (περὶ πάντων ὧν τέτακταί σοι ποιῆσαι), an apparent change—possibly explicatory on Paul's part (cf. τί σε δεῖ ποιεῖν, Acts 9:6)—although, again, Jesus may have said "all that you have been assigned to do" originally, and

---

9. Cf. Schnabel, *Acts*, 902: "Paul begins with an account of his encounter with Jesus of Nazareth on the road to Damascus (vv. 6–11). In verse 6 Luke adds two details to the third person account in 9:3. Both the time reference ('about noon') and the characterization of the light as 'great' provide precise and vivid details appropriate for an eyewitness account in the first person." Cf. similarly David G. Peterson, *The Acts of the Apostles* (Grand Rapids: Eerdmans, 2009), 599.

Luke conveyed the idea more briefly in Acts 9.[10] Once, Paul recounts words spoken by him but not recorded in the Acts 9 account: "'What shall I do, Lord?' I asked."[11] Moreover, and perhaps most importantly for his audience's sake, Paul's recounting of the light has an implicitly evangelistic purpose: "He focuses here on the 'brightness' or 'glory' (δόξα) of the light that he saw, as he does in 2 Cor 4:4, where he describes his (and all believers') experience of conversion to faith in Jesus as seeing 'the light of the gospel that displays the glory of Christ (τῆς δόξης τοῦ Χριστοῦ), who is the image of God.'"[12]

It seems the differences between Luke's earlier account and Paul's later retelling are no less egregious than the differences between Moses' earlier account of the Lord's commands in Genesis 2

---

10. This view may be preferable, if one does not want to think Paul attributed words to the Lord that the Lord had not said. Regarding the addition "of Nazareth," cf. Schnabel, *Acts*, 902: "Here the speaker from heaven identifies himself as 'Jesus of Nazareth' ... an addition that is appropriate for the setting of the speech before a Jewish audience" Cf. likewise I. Howard Marshall, *The Acts of the Apostles: An Introduction and Commentary* (Leicester: Inter-Varsity Press, 1980), 355. Regarding the addition, "Damascus," and the change, "all that you have been assigned to do," in verse 10 cf. likewise Schnabel, *Acts*, 903: "With these additions Paul underlines two facts: the full scope of what he has been doing in his ministry, without exception, has been assigned to him, and his activities are divine orders, not his subjective, individualistic choice." Cf. similarly Simon J. Kistemaker, *Exposition of the Acts of the Apostles*, New Testament Commentary (Grand Rapids: Baker, 1990), 786: "The earlier account (9:5–7) differs slightly from the description Paul gives before his Jewish audience, for *he supplies them with additional information* [emphasis added]. First, Paul relates that the men who accompanied him 'saw the light.' Next, Paul reveals a continued dialogue with Jesus. He asked him, 'What shall I do, Lord?' This question and the sentence that introduces Jesus' response are lacking in the first report of Paul's conversion. And last, the instructions Jesus gave are more detailed in the second account than in the first. The clause *everything that has been arranged for you* has been added."

11. Against the objection that the use of "Lord [κύριος]" in verse 10 would be improper before a Jewish audience, cf. Ernst Haenchen, *The Acts of the Apostles: A Commentary* (Philadelphia: Westminster, 1971), 626, who states: "Luke is thinking about his readers, not about Paul's listeners." I prefer to take Luke's record of Paul's account in Acts 22 as historically accurate, without imposing any assumptions as to how Luke may have modified it.

12. Schnabel, *Acts*, 904.

and the woman's retelling of them in Genesis 3.[13] If one wants to see theological significance in the woman's version, one can also find them in Paul's version: the pointedly theophanic brightness of the light and the more explicit "all that you have been assigned to do."

If one does not fault Paul for seemingly exaggerating what happened or for attributing words to the Lord that he did not in fact say, how can one fault the woman for "minimizing" God's permissions and attributing words to the Lord that he did not in fact say? A simpler and apparently better way to view both examples would be to accept the laconic nature of reporting and understand that the earlier account in each case gives less information about the event, while the later recounting in each case gives additional information not provided in the earlier account.[14]

ACTS 26

Paul's account of his Damascus road experience in the presence of Festus and Agrippa appears to supply still more information when compared with the accounts in Acts 9 and Acts 22. Although some scholars have thought it contradicts the two previous accounts, a review may indicate that it does not really contradict those accounts but adds to what can be learned from them. As before, differences between the accounts are in italics.

---

13. The fact that Paul was an eyewitness reporter and the woman in Gen 3:1 reports what Adam (apparently) had told her makes no real difference, unless one also wants to fault Adam with giving the woman an inaccurate report. What matters is the difference between the first and second accounts recorded by the historian in each case.

14. All reporting is probably laconic to some degree, either because the author does not have all possible relevant data or because of selectivity on the author's part. Anyone who has written an article or a book is familiar with these realities. The same applies in everyday experience, whether it involves online or broadcast media, or newspaper or journal reports.

Acts 26:13–20

"About noon, King Agrippa, as I was on the road, I saw *a light from heaven, brighter than the sun, blazing around me and my companions. We all fell* to the ground, and I heard a voice *saying to me in Aramaic, 'Saul, Saul, why do you persecute me? It is hard for you to kick against the goads.'*

"Then I asked, 'Who are you, Lord?'

"'I am Jesus, whom you are persecuting,' the Lord replied. 'Now get up and *stand on your feet. I have appeared to you to appoint you as a servant and as a witness of what you have seen and will see of me. I will rescue you from your own people and from the Gentiles. I am sending you to them to open their eyes and turn them from darkness to light, and from the power of Satan to God, so that they may receive forgiveness of sins and a place among those who are sanctified by faith in me.'*

"*So then, King Agrippa, I was not disobedient to the vision from heaven. First to those in Damascus, then to those in Jerusalem and in all Judea, and then to the Gentiles, I preached that they should repent and turn to God and demonstrate their repentance by their deeds."*

Paul adds to or clarifies the earlier reports in the following ways:

Acts 9 Luke's account	Acts 22 Paul's recounting	Acts 26 Paul's recounting
³ As	⁶ About noon	¹³ About noon
a light from heaven	a bright light from heaven	a light from heaven, brighter than the sun
flashed around him	flashed around me	blazing around me and my companions

Acts 9 Luke's account	Acts 22 Paul's recounting	Acts 26 Paul's recounting
⁴ He fell to the ground	⁷ I fell to the ground	¹⁴ We all fell to the ground
a voice say to him	a voice say to me	a voice saying to me
		in Aramaic, "Saul, Saul, why do you persecute me? It is hard for you to kick against the goads."
⁵ "I am Jesus"	⁸ "I am Jesus of Nazareth"	¹⁵ "I am Jesus"
"whom you are persecuting"	"whom you are persecuting"	"whom you are persecuting"
	¹⁰ "What shall I do, Lord?" I asked.	
⁶ "Now get up"	"Get up"	¹⁶ "Now get up"
"and go into the city"	"and go into Damascus"	"and stand on your feet"
"and you will be told what you must do" (ὅ τί σε δεῖ ποιεῖν)	"and there you will be told all that you have been assigned to do" (lit., "what it behooves you to do")	"I have appeared to you to appoint you as a servant and as a witness of what you have seen and will see of me"

Acts 9 Luke's account	Acts 22 Paul's recounting	Acts 26 Paul's recounting
		[17] "I will rescue you from your own people and from the Gentiles. I am sending you to them [18] to open their eyes and turn them from darkness to light, and from the power of Satan to God, so that they may receive forgiveness of sins and a place among those who are sanctified by faith in me."
[8] when he opened his eyes he could see nothing. So they led ...	[11] the brilliance of the light had blinded me. My companions led ...	[19] So then, King Agrippa, I was not disobedient to the vision from heaven.
		[20] First to those in Damascus, then to those in Jerusalem and in all Judea, and then to the Gentiles, I preached that they should repent and turn to God and demonstrate their repentance by their deeds.

It does not appear that Paul's account to Festus and Agrippa (as reported by Luke) contradicts Luke's earlier account (in Acts 9) or Paul's reported account before the Jews in Jerusalem (in Acts 22). Nonetheless it may be helpful to consider the differences in detail, in order to make the lack of contradiction clear, because not all scholars have seen it so.[15] What then are the differences, and what significance do they have?

The first difference is that Paul now gives a fuller description of the theophanic event. The light is now more fully described: it was "brighter than the sun, blazing around me and my companions" (Acts 26:13). Both the brightness of the light and the extent of its effulgence are more fully portrayed. There is no need to see the differences as anything more than additional data.[16] The second difference is that, whereas in the first two accounts it was only Paul who "fell to the ground," in the last account Paul says, "We all fell to the ground" (v. 14). This difference may also be seen as additional data. There is no compelling reason to see any contradiction here (after all, "We all fell to the ground" is inclusive of "I fell to the ground," and "I fell to the ground" is not exclusive of "We all fell to the ground"), and the objection made by some that Paul, because he was blinded, could not have seen whether others also fell to the ground is hardly compelling.[17] Paul could have learned this detail from his companions shortly after the event.[18]

---

15. For instance, Kirsopp Lake and Henry J. Cadbury, *The Acts of the Apostles*, part I, vol. IV of *The Beginnings of Christianity*, ed. F. J. Foakes Jackson and Kirsopp Lake (London: Macmillan and Co., 1933), 101, see a conflict between Acts 9:4 ("He fell to the ground") and 26:14 ("We all fell to the ground"), calling it "a ... formal but unimportant contradiction."

16. As Schnabel, *Acts*, 1008, appropriately notes, the expression, "brighter than the sun ... highlights the supernatural origin of the phenomenon."

17. For one exponent of that view, see Ben Witherington III, *The Acts of the Apostles: A Socio-Rhetorical Commentary* (Grand Rapids: Eerdmans, 1998), 312.

18. Many commentators have recognized the possibility that Acts 26:14 reports a detail not mentioned in the earlier accounts. The narrative in Acts 26 could refer to

Next, Paul's final account does not mention the Lord's instruction to go into Damascus but does add that the Lord said, "Stand on your feet" (v. 16). Finally, the Lord's commission (vv. 15–18) is much more extensively reported than it was in either of the earlier reports. Nothing in it, however, contradicts the earlier reports. Maybe Paul telescopes into this summary account the instruction he had— from Jesus, indeed—via Ananias, as Witherington has suggested.[19] This seems likely since Paul does not mention Ananias at all in his account before Festus and Agrippa, and this may be for the sake of conciseness or perhaps even to protect Ananias and others in Damascus from any possible negative official repercussions (e.g., persecution or prosecution) later.[20] In that case he reports the Lord's words given to him through another, just as, long before, the woman had reported the Lord's words given to her by her husband, Adam. The essentials of the chain of communication—the Lord to one human, and that human to another human—are the same, even if Adam conveyed to his wife words he had heard audibly (presumably) and Ananias conveyed to Paul words he had from the Lord, although one cannot know whether by external or internal audition. Indeed, we are in no position to say precisely how each prophet— Adam and Ananias—received his words from the Lord. It may be,

---

the immediate effect of the appearance of the light. Saul and his companions were suddenly struck to the ground together. This was before the voice spoke to Saul. In Acts 9:7 the historian is speaking of what occurred after that first impact: Saul's companions (who were not as directly and intimately impacted by the theophany as was Saul, for whom it was intended) got up from the ground but stood speechless. Cf. Schnabel, *Acts*, 1008, "If this is not simply a stylistic variation, Luke emphasizes the witness that Paul's companions could provide concerning the event."

19. Witherington, *The Acts of the Apostles*, 312. Cf. Schnabel, *Acts*, 1009, who also notes this possibility.

20. Barrett, *A Critical and Exegetical Commentary*, 443–44, suggests regarding Paul's failure to mention Ananias: "It is understandable that for Paul himself the appearance and presence of Christ were so commanding that secondary actors in the story scarcely counted and did not have to be mentioned."

however, that Paul now reports most fully what the glorified Jesus had said to him on the road, a possibility discussed by Schnabel:

> Paul provides in 26:15–18 the historically clearest report of his commission: according to his own words in Gal 1:1, 15–16, he did not receive his commission from human beings but directly from God; the words of Ananias in Acts 22:14–15 may allude to Paul's commission on the road to Damascus, whose significance Ananias explains to Paul, while the report concerning Ananias's involvement in 9:10–17 also does not speak of a commissioning of Paul by Ananias. Luke may have been saving this important detail of Paul's conversion and commission for maximum effect in Paul's speech before King Agrippa.[21]

It seems unlikely that anyone will provide conclusive evidence as to whether Paul telescopes the data or reports Jesus' words as he heard them on the road to Damascus. In either case, it seems fairly clear that one has in the Acts 26 account an example of earlier laconic reporting supplemented by a later account.

One detail deserves special attention. It has been objected that the saying, "It is hard for you to kick against the goads" (v. 14), was originally a Greek saying that Paul used in order to convey his message more effectively.[22] That view, however, flatly contradicts Paul's

---

21. Schnabel, *Acts*, 1009. Cf. also Charles W. Hedrick, "Paul's Conversion/Call: A Comparative Analysis of the Three Reports in Acts," *JBL* 100.3 (1981): 415–32, 427.

22. As Schnabel, *Acts*, 1008, notes, "This reference has been explained as Paul's attempt to clarify the implications of the question of the heavenly voice for his Greek-oriented audience." He appropriately observes: "To interpret the 'pricks' of the goad in terms of Paul's conscience, popularly often related to Paul's memory of his part in Stephen's death, is not plausible since Paul's references to his preconversion period do not indicate any pangs of conscience (cf. Acts 26:19–11; Gal. 1:13–14; Phil. 3:5–6" (*Acts*, 1008n76).

claim that the *Lord said* that to him "in Aramaic."[23] Witherington, for example, has argued:

> This expression was a *Greek* not Jewish idiom, and it meant "It is fruitless to struggle against God, or against one's destiny." This proverbial saying was one that Agrippa or Festus would likely have understood and perhaps even heard before ... but it is hardly something one would expect to originate on the lips of Jesus in Aramaic. Paul or Luke inserts this line into the discourse to make clear that Jesus had indicated to Paul that he was struggling against God by persecuting Christians, and indeed against his own destiny. The phrase, which Jesus surely did not use when he spoke to Saul originally, indicated to the audience that Paul was pursuing his present mission because God had mandated for him to do so.[24]

This analysis appears, however, to raise several problems. The first is that the saying, which had apparently become proverbial, "is hardly something one would expect to originate on the lips of Jesus in Aramaic." It is a dubious proposition that what we would expect Jesus to say is a standard by which to evaluate a report of what Jesus said. One might also say, for example, that one would hardly expect Jeremiah to deliver a judgment in Aramaic to an audience in Jerusalem (Jer 10:11), or Paul to allude to an expression used by Aristotle when writing to the (apparently Jewish Christian) Romans (Rom 2:14).[25] We have no way of knowing whether the Greek adage,

---

23. Lit., "τῇ Ἑβραΐδι διαλέκτῳ," "in the Hebrew language," most likely Aramaic, since most contemporary Jews spoke Aramaic and not Hebrew; cf. ESV, n. "*the Hebrew dialect* (probably Aramaic)."

24. Witherington, *The Acts of the Apostles*, 311–12. Witherington notes that the idiom occurs in Euripides' *The Bacchae*; "This shows at least Luke's, if not Paul's familiarity with Greek idioms" (*The Acts of the Apostles*, 311n28).

25. Cf. *BT* 2, 338n17. Even today, English speakers who do not know German easily say, "One can't do everything," and the Germans say the same, "Man kann

whose meaning is clear, had not made its way into Aramaic usage, and it was surely not beyond Jesus' *ability* to make the statement to Paul in Aramaic. Moreover, if the claim that Jesus spoke in Aramaic was problematic, why make it? Why tell Festus and Agrippa that Jesus had spoken a Greek adage to him in Aramaic? Furthermore, if Jesus did not use those words, what words did he use? The points Paul makes could have been made without using the phrase in question. Finally, if Jesus did not actually say those words, it may be difficult to see how Paul is being accurate or even truthful in his report. He appears to be attributing words to the Lord that the Lord did not say. Or, if Paul did not say this to Festus and Agrippa, then Luke is attributing to Paul, and also to the Lord, words that neither of them said.

OVERALL CONCLUSION
REGARDING ACTS DATA

A review of the parallel accounts in Acts 9, 22, and 26 suggests that the three accounts are consistent and that what some have seen as contradictions need not be seen as such. Statements that appear at first glance to be contradictory in a later account can equally well be seen as the provision of supplementary or clarifying information.

The existence of these parallel accounts in Luke's history does not ipso facto present itself as a hermeneutical key or interpretive aid to understanding the parallels between Genesis 2:17 and Genesis 3:3. On the other hand, the sequence of accounts in Acts does have some narrative and historiographic features in common with those that have been seen in Genesis, including not only the Genesis 2 and Genesis 3 parallel but also the parallels between Genesis 12 and Genesis 20 and between the Abrahamic narrative

---

nicht alles tun." Different languages that have geographical or historical affinity can also use shared or borrowed phraseology.

material in Genesis 12–22 and the Lord's statement to Isaac in Genesis 26:5. The resultant picture may be outlined as follows:

Case #1

1. In Genesis 2 the historian Moses records what the Lord God said to Adam regarding the trees.

2. In Genesis 3 the woman recounts to an audience (the serpent) what God had said, with additional detail.

Case #2

1. In Genesis 12 the historian Moses records what Abram told Sarai to say (to Pharaoh)—that she was his sister.

2. In Genesis 20 Abraham recounts to an audience (Abimelech) what he had told Sarai to say (to anyone)—that she was his sister.

Case #3

1. In Genesis 12–22 the historian Moses records whatever the Lord commanded Abraham.

2. In Genesis 26:5 the Lord recounts to an audience (Isaac), in more detail, what he had commanded Abraham—"My charge, My commandments, My statutes, and My laws."

Case #4

1. In Acts 9 the historian Luke records what the Lord said in theophany to Paul, and what followed.

2. In Acts 22 Paul recounts to an audience (the Jews) in more detail what the Lord had said in theophany, and what followed.

3. In Acts 26 Paul recounts to an audience (Festus and Agrippa) in yet more detail what the Lord had said in theophany, and what followed.

These four cases appear to offer a parallel pattern:

1. First, the historian records a situation with one or more commands in a third-person omniscient narrative.

2. Later, an individual who was part of the situation recounts the earlier event and earlier command(s), with more detail, in a first-person narrative.

In each case of subsequent, first-person recounting, the individual adds supplemental and/or clarifying details. This is true, whether the first-person speaker *received* the commands (as was the case of the woman in Gen 3 and of Paul in Acts 22 and 26) or *gave* the commands (as was the case of Abraham, who "commanded" Sarah, as per Gen 20, and of the Lord, who commanded Abraham, as per Gen 26).

Moses and Luke were two different historians with very different backgrounds and milieus. Each had different tasks assigned him by the Lord. But among those tasks, each was led to compose historical material. Broadly speaking, Moses was led to compose the human background in the world—and also the career—of the covenant mediator (namely, himself), as well as the cutting of the old covenant (in the Pentateuch). Luke was led to compose the human background in the world (including the otherworldly source)—and also the career—of the covenant mediator (namely, Jesus), as well as the cutting of the new covenant (in Luke's Gospel). Moses was led to compose the history of God's people for some time (in Exodus 21–Deuteronomy) after the old covenant was cut. Luke was led to compose the history of God's people for some time (in Acts) after the new covenant was cut.

In God's providence both historians had occasion to report events laconically in third-person omniscient narratives, supplemented by later accounts of the same events reported in the first person by people involved in those earlier scenarios. The present work proposes that such a view of narrative sequence is the appropriate way to understand the contrast between the third-person omniscient account of Genesis 2:17 compared with the first-person account in Genesis 3:3. On such an understanding, the woman would not appear to have added to or altered (in Gen 3:2–3) what the Lord had said to Adam (in Gen 2:16–17).

Epilogue

WHAT COMES NEXT?

This monograph, qua monograph, has been limited in scope. That is so even though it has explored passages beyond Genesis 3 by way of comparative study and drawn on representative scholarship that addresses those passages. I have chosen comparisons that, I hope, adequately illustrate the proposal made at the outset of this study and also undergird it sufficiently to show it has some standing and is worthy of recognition and hopefully adoption by others.

The monograph has explored one phenomenon located and demonstrated in the realm of biblical historiography. Other examples of this sort can likely be found. Other issues pertaining to biblical historiography and how it both resembles and differs from ancient Near Eastern historiography—or more particularly historiography as practiced by, e.g., Egypt, Babylon, Hatti, or Assyria—still constitute potentially fruitful areas of study. This is true regarding biblical historiography in general, whether the subject be the Old Testament or the New Testament. There is a world of difference, for instance, between Thucydides or Polybius or Suetonius and the Pentateuch or Luke–Acts, and the reason, it has been proposed, is the same for Luke and the other Gospel writers as it is for the Old Testament history writers: God in covenantal relation informs the Old Testament and New Testament histories and biblical history overall, and that difference in dynamic reality inevitably produces different ways of writing history. That is why I have called the Bible in a summary fashion "the annals of the Great King."

One thing I would propose regarding biblical historiography is that it is never propaganda: It never seeks to persuade us of a merely human point of view. It is always, to use the German term, *sachgemäß*. I hope the present work is worthy of the same judgment.

CONCLUDING THEOLOGICAL POSTSCRIPT

Although Genesis 2:17 and 3:2–3 are part of Genesis, and Genesis is part of the Mosaic corpus (the Pentateuch), and the Pentateuch is part of the Old Testament, and the Old Testament is part of the Bible, as is the book of Acts, which has also come under consideration in the present work—although these things are true, and although the Bible is the foundation of all true theology, the present work has been primarily historiographical and not theological.

Nonetheless, the material that forms the basis of the present study does afford some scope for theology, although that scope is limited if we restrict ourselves to the verses mentioned. There are at least three possible roads of theological inquiry that arise from study of those verses alone.

THE TREE OF LIFE AND THAT OTHER TREE: WHAT TO EAT AND WHEN TO EAT?

One avenue of theological inquiry has to do with the nature of the two trees. Subsumed under that topic would be the question, "Did Adam and his wife, before the fall, have the privilege of eating regularly from the tree of life, or was that prerogative reserved to them in case they successfully rebuffed the serpent?" Traditional Reformed theology has thought the latter and therefore named the tree of the knowledge of good and evil a "judgment tree," with the understanding that Adam and his wife would be judged according to their behavior regarding that tree and also that the serpent would be judged with regard to that tree if Adam and his wife rejected the serpent's temptation to eat from that tree. If they passed the test, they would get to eat from the tree of life and live forever.

The idea that Adam and his wife could eat from the tree of life only after passing the test of rebuffing the snake—which would be their probationary event—may find support in the way the Lord God speaks of the second tree: "In the day that you eat of it you shall surely die" (Gen 2:17b NKJV). The issue here is not what "in the day" means. Rather, the issue is that eating from the tree of the knowledge of good and evil *only once* guaranteed death. By analogy, then, eating from the tree of life *only once* might guarantee life. That would fit well with the feel of what the Lord says just before he expels them from Eden: "And now, lest he put out his hand and take also of the tree of life, and eat, and live forever" (Gen 3:22b NKJV). That statement certainly gives the impression that one would live forever if one ate from the tree of life only once and the concomitant impression that Adam and his wife had not yet eaten from the tree of life.

There does appear to be evidence of an alternate possibility, however. The Lord God had told Adam: "Of every tree of the garden you may freely eat; but of the tree of the knowledge of good and evil you shall not eat" (Gen 2:16–17a NKJV). That is, the Lord gave Adam permission to eat from *every tree of the garden except one*. The Lord forbade eating from the tree of the knowledge of good and evil. The Lord *did not forbid eating from the tree of life*. That raises the possibility that Adam and his wife were free to eat from the tree of life even before the serpent showed up. In that case, eating from the tree of life regularly might sustain life indefinitely, until the Lord chose to provide some other way of instituting eternal life.[1]

A related question would have to do with aging: Would Adam and his wife have lived forever but nonetheless continued to grow older? Greek and Roman mythology offer the case of Tithonus, a prince of Troy chosen by Eos (Roman "Aurora"), goddess of the dawn, to be her lover. She asked Zeus (Roman "Jupiter") to grant him eternal life but forgot to ask Zeus to grant him eternal youth. When Tithonus became too old to move, Eos locked him in his chamber. Eventually, she turned him into a grasshopper.[2] Entertaining as such a myth may be, the Bible makes it clear that, even after the fall, the Lord graciously sustained very long human life spans until he withdrew that form of his Spirit's support just before the flood (Gen 6:3). That later information may suggest that it was the work of the Spirit somehow to sustain human life, even if the Spirit would have worked in some manner through the tree of life. Genesis 2–3 says nothing of possible aging before the fall, but since Adam and his wife were to have children (Gen 1:28) who would grow up and subdue the earth as part of the cultural mandate, aging would seem to have been part of God's plan for humans, even before the fall and without death.

Beyond that fairly reasonable understanding, one might assume, as Kline does, some sort of heavenizing of humans and the world—some ultimate transformation into a truly eternal state, had the first Adam been obedient.[3] Since he was not, the Second Adam will accomplish the transformation at the eschaton (cf. Rev 21:2).

---

1. See discussion above, chapter 3; see also fuller discussion in *BT* 2, 14–15.

2. See Thomas Bulfinch, *The Age of Fable, or, Beauties of Mythology* (Philadelphia: David McKay, 1898), 258.

3. Meredith G. Kline, *God, Heaven, and Har Magedon: A Covenantal Tale of Cosmos and Telos* (Eugene, OR: Wipf & Stock, 2006); cf. Niehaus, *BT* 2, 16.

WHEN DID EVE SIN?

A proposal that underlies this work is that one must understand faith if one is to understand sin. That is so because Paul has said, "Whatever is not from faith is sin" (Rom 14:23 NASB). If faith is amening God, as has been argued, then whatever does not amen God—whatever is not on the same page as God—is sin.

It would follow that the woman could not have been going adrift, zealously overstating God's command, or overstating it out of a sense that she found his actual command too hard, and thus overstated its hardness, when she answered the serpent's question. It is also impossible to prove that she misremembered what Adam had told her of God's command and equally impossible to prove that Adam, for whatever reason, had misinformed her of God's command. And since no amount of analysis can, unfortunately, reveal her state of mind when she answered the serpent, the interpreter is faced with a choice: either add one of the considerations just mentioned as an interpretive guess, or conclude that she was most likely adding information to an earlier laconic account of the Lord's command (in Gen 2:17b) when she answered the serpent's question (Gen 3:3b).

If one asks when the woman did sin, the Bible provides an obvious answer: "The woman … was deceived and became a sinner" (1 Tim 2:14b). The woman was ensnared by the deceptiveness of sin (Heb 3:13), and at that moment she became a sinner *in her thoughts*. Next, she took the fruit and ate it, and became a sinner *in her act*. This sequence of events has become all too human, and it is no doubt against this very thing that Paul affirms, with an implicit exhortation: "We demolish arguments and every pretension that sets itself up against the knowledge of God, and we take captive every thought to make it obedient to Christ" (2 Cor 10:5).

James also addresses this sequence, emphasizing sin as action that results from thought: "But each person is tempted when he is

lured and enticed by his own desire. Then desire when it has conceived gives birth to sin, and sin when it is fully grown brings forth
death" (Jas 1:14–15 ESV). James is not telling us that bad desires are not
sin, however. Paul has affirmed that we take every thought captive
to obey Christ. The same statement makes it clear that thoughts
can disobey Christ, and such thoughts—which would include the
sorts of desires James mentioned, and the sort of desire Adam's wife
conceived—are by definition sin since all sin is disobedience to God,
also characterized as "lawlessness" (1 John 3:4). When the woman
began to covet the fruit of the tree of the knowledge of good and
evil, she was already sinning in her heart and mind (cf. the Tenth
commandment, "You shall not *covet* your neighbor's house. You
shall not *covet* your neighbor's wife," etc., Exod 20:17, emphases
added). Then, her sinful desire led to her sinful act.

The woman's progress from innocence to sinfulness, as reported
by Scripture, illustrates what has been said above. The first report
of her thoughts (as contrasted to her words in Gen 3:2–3) portray
the very transition from sin in her thoughts (i.e., desire) to sin in
her act (i.e., taking and eating the fruit): "When the woman saw
that the fruit of the tree was good for food and pleasing to the eye,
and also *desirable* for gaining wisdom, she took some and ate it"
(Gen 3:6, emphasis added). She drifted into sinful thought because
of the mystery of deception: "The serpent deceived me, and I ate"
(Gen 3:13).

One should be clear that when she thought the fruit was "desirable," she was already sinning in her thoughts. A train of thought
obedient to what the Lord commanded would not find the fruit
desirable, because its desirability lay in its prospect of providing
wisdom in a way God had forbidden ("*desirable* for gaining wisdom").
To an obedient way of thinking, nothing could be desirable about
gaining wisdom in a way God had forbidden.

HOW DOES A SINLESS
BEING FALL INTO SIN?

At least one question remains to be asked: How does a sinless being fall into sin? For her part, the woman confesses what she knows: "The serpent deceived me, and I ate" (Gen 3:13). Deception, then, would appear to lie at the foundation of sin. Hebrews affirms that understanding: "But encourage one another daily, as long as it is called 'Today,' so that none of you may be hardened by sin's deceitfulness" (Heb 3:13). The object of such encouragement would be faith (cf. Rom 1:11–12, "I long to see you so that I may impart to you some spiritual gift to make you strong—that is, that you and I may be mutually encouraged by each other's faith"). We encourage one another in the Lord, which means we contribute to that courage which adheres to a life of faith, a life of amening God. By doing so, we avoid "sin's deceitfulness."

If sin is inherently deceitful, what does that mean? One explanation would be that, since we were made for God, and since God is good, and since everything he created was originally "very good" (Gen 1:31), then whatever God created for humans was meant to be good for them. Sin perverts this by falsely presenting what is not good as though it were good. This is exactly what the serpent did with the woman. He convinced her that the fruit of that tree was good in several ways ("the tree was good for food and pleasing to the eye, and also *desirable* for gaining wisdom," Gen 3:6), but chiefly, that it was good ("desirable") to make one wise. To use the language of Hebrews, when the woman became convinced that the tree had those qualities (i.e., when she fell victim to "sin's deceitfulness")—and, most of all, when she became convinced that it was "desirable for gaining wisdom"—she became a sinner.

I have used the expression "the mystery of deception" as an attempt to capture this idea, because it is mysterious how a person can be deceived into thinking what has been forbidden by a good

God can, nonetheless, be good. It would seem to be especially mysterious how a sinless being, such as the woman before her fall, could be deceived into such a view of things, which was diametrically opposed to the truth. Clearly the serpent persuaded her, but how can one explain her inner dynamics as she responded favorably to that persuasion? The sad thing is, all people have experienced sin and the deceptions that lead to it, even if the most thoughtful people cannot explain how it happens. Even Paul expressed how frustrating and inscrutable such life experiences were for a man under the law, which exposed the hidden nature of sin but could not give one the power to overcome it (cf. Rom 7:7–25).

CONCLUDING THOUGHTS:
THE SERPENT

Although the serpent was the instigator of the events that led to the composition of this book, he has not been the focus of the present work. Nonetheless some remarks on his own sinfulness and, in particular, how he came to be "that ancient serpent, called the devil, or Satan" (Rev 12:9) and "the father of lies" (John 8:44) may not be out of place. Since the question of sin's genesis in the woman has been raised, the same question regarding the serpent may also be raised: How did a sinless being (Lucifer, untarnished) fall into sin?

Not everyone will agree as to what biblical materials could form evidence that bears on this question. One long-held view has been that the portrayals of the king of Babylon in Isaiah 14 and of the prince of Tyre in Ezekiel 28 adumbrate, symbolically represent, or show fallen humans who embody to some extent, the characteristics of Satan as he is later more fully revealed in the New Testament.[4]

---

4. It is worth noting that Isaiah is told regarding the material in question that God's people will one day "take up this taunt against the king of Babylon" (Isa 14:4). The word translated "taunt" is Hebrew מָשָׁל, and it means basically a comparison. In other words, the king of Babylon may implicitly be compared to another entity, and,

If one proceeds on that assumption, then a desire to be like "the Most High" (Isa 14:14, cf. vv. 13–14), which resulted from his pride in his own splendor (Ezek 28:17, cf. vv. 13–17), led to his downfall. The irony here is that he, who wanted to be like God, tempted the woman with the same temptation. It is relevant to this interpretation that the king of Babylon is called "Lucifer" in Isaiah (Isa 14:12, Vulgate), and the prince of Tyre is said to have been a guardian cherub in Eden in Ezekiel (Ezek 28:13–14).

If that view of the matter is correct, then one could suggest that the one now known as Satan became, before he lost his splendor, conceited about his own glory. He would have done what Paul implicitly advises against: "We do not dare to classify or compare ourselves with some who commend themselves. When they *measure themselves by themselves* and *compare themselves with themselves*, they are not wise" (2 Cor 10:12, emphases added). Perhaps Lucifer, before his fall, measured himself by himself and compared himself with himself, and so worked himself up into an inflated view of himself. An older meaning of the word "conceit" characterizes this way of thinking: in Shakespeare's day, a "conceit" was an exaggerated idea built up in one's mind, and this could be an exaggerated idea of oneself.[5] In this view, Lucifer became conceited.

A hint of an additional possibility, consistent with what has just been said, may appear in Paul's advice regarding appointment of overseers: "He must not be a recent convert, or he may become

---

on the present interpretation, that entity (namely, Satan) would be much greater and more powerful than any human king, although evil human kings and rulers may in their pretentions resemble him, who is in a sense their archetype.

5. Cf. https://www.etymonline.com/word/conceit: "late 14c., 'a thought, a notion, that which is mentally conceived,' from conceiven (see conceive) based on analogy of deceit/deceive and receipt/receive. Sense evolved from 'something formed in the mind' to 'fanciful or witty notion, ingenious thought' (1510s), to 'vanity, exaggerated estimate of one's own mental abilities' (c. 1600) through shortening of self-conceit (1580s)."

conceited and fall under the same judgment as the devil. He must also have a good reputation with outsiders, so that he will not fall into disgrace and into the devil's trap" (1 Tim 3:6–7). One could imagine a sinless being, such as Satan before his sin, becoming conceited by a series of incremental false reasonings about his own glory. As Ezekiel's prophecy about the prince of Tyre (the guardian cherub in Eden) explains: "Your heart became proud on account of your beauty, and you corrupted your wisdom because of your splendor" (Ezek 28:17).[6]

Supposing Lucifer/Satan fell from heaven (although apparently with visitation rights to the heavenly court, cf. Job 1–2), how did he become a serpent? Since Revelation 12:9 identifies him as such, he is understood to have appeared in that form in Genesis 3. Two possibilities immediately come to mind: (1) he took the form of a serpent in order to astonish the woman and perhaps, taking advantage of her surprise, lend credence to his counsel; (2) he possessed a serpent and used it for that same purpose. Either of these seems possible, and neither can be proved. In either case, one might question God's fairness in issuing a harsh judgment against an animal that was abused by the enemy and had no choice in the matter. But it may help to recall Jesus' judgment against a fig tree because it did not provide fruit when he looked for fruit from it (John 21:18–19). That may have been a symbolic case: as the fig tree did not bear fruit for its Creator when it should have and was condemned to be fruitless henceforth, so Israel had not born the expected fruit for its Creator and would be likewise condemned (cf. the prophetic covenant lawsuit parable, Isa 5:1–7). If God could, with a symbolic purpose, condemn a fruit tree, he could likewise condemn a snake.

---

6. Cf. discussion in Niehaus, *BT* 3, 139.

BIBLIOGRAPHY

Alexander, T. D. "Are the Wife/Sister Incidents of Genesis Literary
    Compositional Variants?" *VT* XLII.2 (1992): 145–53.

Alford, Henry. *The Book of Genesis*. Minneapolis: Kirk & Kirk, 1872.

Ambrose. *Hexameron, Paradise, and Cain and Abel*. Translated by
    John J. Savage. The Fathers of the Church 42. Washington,
    DC: The Catholic University of America Press, 1961.

Atkinson, Basil F. C. *The Book of Genesis*. Chicago: Moody Press,
    1957.

Augustine. *On Genesis: Two Books on Genesis against the Manichees,
    and On the Literal Interpretation of Genesis: An Unfinished
    Book*. Translated by Roland J. Teske, SJ. The Fathers of the
    Church 84. Washington, DC: The Catholic University of
    America Press, 1991.

Baron, Christopher A. "Greek Historiography." In *Oxford
    Bibliographies*. http://www.oxfordbibliographies.com/view/
    document/obo-9780195389661/obo-9780195389661-0078
    .xml.

Barrett, C. K. *A Critical and Exegetical Commentary on the Acts of
    the Apostles, Volume 1*. International Critical Commentary.
    Edinburgh: T&T Clark, 1994.

Barth, Karl. *Church Dogmatics* III, 3: *The Doctrine of Creation*.
    Translated by G. W. Bromiley and R. J. Ehrlich.
    Edinburgh: T&T Clark, 1960.

———. *Kirchliche Dogmatik* III, 3: *Die Lehre von der Schöpfung*. Zollikon-Zürich: Evangelischer Verlag A.G., 1950.

Bate, Walter Jackson. *From Classic to Romantic: Premises of Taste in Eighteenth Century England*. Cambridge: Harvard University Press, 1946.

Beale, G. K. *New Testament Biblical Theology*. Grand Rapids: Baker Academic, 2011.

Bock, Darrell L. *Acts*. Grand Rapids: Baker Academic, 2007.

Bonhoeffer, Dietrich. *Creation and Fall*. In *The Bonhoeffer Reader*. Edited by Clifford J. Green and Michael P. DeJonge. Minneapolis: Fortress, 2013.

———. *Creation and Fall: A Theological Interpretation of Genesis 1–3*. In *Creation and Fall & Temptation: Two Biblical Studies*. Translated by John C. Fletcher. New York: Macmillan, 1963.

Brown, Francis, Samuel Rolles Driver, and Charles A. Briggs. *A Hebrew and English Lexicon of the Old Testament*. Oxford: Clarendon, 1904.

Bulfinch, Thomas. *The Age of Fable, or, Beauties of Mythology*. Philadelphia: David McKay, 1898.

Calvin, John. *Commentaries on the First Book of Moses Called Genesis, Volume First*. Translated by Rev. John King. Grand Rapids: Eerdmans, 1948.

Cassuto, Umberto. *A Commentary on the Book of Genesis, Part One: From Adam to Noah, Gen I–VI 8*. Translated by Israel Abrahams. Jerusalem: Magnes, 1961.

———. *The Documentary Hypothesis*. Jerusalem: Magnes, 1983.

"The Chicago Statement on Biblical Inerrancy." Accessed January 10, 2020. http://www.danielakin.com/wp-content/uploads/old/Resource_545/Book%202,%20Sec%2023.pdf.

Childs, Brevard S. *Biblical Theology in Crisis*. Philadelphia: Westminster, 1970.

————. *Biblical Theology of the Old and New Testaments: Theological Reflection on the Christian Bible*. Philadelphia: Fortress, 1993.

Clines, David J. A., and John Elwolde, eds. *Yodh-Lamedh*. Vols. 4 & 6 of *The Dictionary of Classical Hebrew*. Sheffield: Sheffield Academic Press, 1998.

Conant, Thomas J. *The Book of Genesis*. New York: American Bible Union, 1868.

Conzelmann, Hans. *Acts of the Apostles*. Translated by James Limburg, A. Thomas Kraabel, and Donald H. Juel. Philadelphia: Fortress, 1987.

Dillmann, A. *Die Genesis*. 6th ed. Leipzig: Hirzel, 1892.

————. *Genesis Critically and Exegetically Expounded*. Vol. 1. Translated by Wm. B. Stevenson. Edinburgh: T&T Clark, 1897.

Dods, Marcus. *Genesis*. Edinburgh: T&T Clark, 1905.

Driver, S. R. *The Book of Genesis with Introduction and Notes*. London: Methuen & Co. Ltd., 1904.

Ellicott, C. J. *A Bible Commentary for English Readers*. Vol. 1. London: Cassell, 1905.

Gill, John. *Exposition of the Bible*. https://www.biblestudytools.com/commentaries/gills-exposition-of-the-bible/genesis-20-13.html.

————. *An Exposition of the First Book of Moses Called Genesis*. 1778, 1810. Repr., Springfield: Particular Baptist Press, 2010.

Gunkel, Hermann. *Genesis Translated and Interpreted*. Translated by Mark E. Biddle. Macon, GA: Mercer University Press, 1997.

————. *Genesis übersetzt und erklärt*. Göttingen: Vandenhoeck & Ruprecht, 1901.

————. *The Legends of Genesis*. Translated by W. H. Carruth. Chicago: Open Court, 1901.

Haenchen, Ernst. *The Acts of the Apostles: A Commentary*. Philadelphia: Westminster, 1971.

Hedrick, Charles W. "Paul's Conversion/Call: A Comparative Analysis of the Three Reports in Acts." *JBL* 100.3 (1981): 415–32.

Hirsch, Emanuel. "Die Drei Berichte der Apostelgeschichte über die Bekehrung des Paulus." *ZNW* 28 (1929): 305–12.

Holladay, William. *A Concise Hebrew and Aramaic Lexicon of the Old Testament*. Grand Rapids: Eerdmans, 1971.

Jacob, Benno. *Das erste Buch der Tora, Genesis. Übersetzt und erklärt*. Berlin: Schocken, 1934.

———. Ernest I. Jacob and Walter Jacob, trans. *The First Book of the Bible, Genesis*. New York: KTAV, 1974.

Jenni, Ernst. "Das Wort ōlām im Alten Testament," *ZAW*, Band 64, 1952 (Berlin: Töpelmann, 1953): 197–248.

———. "Das Wort ōlām im Alten Testament," continued in *ZAW* 65, 1953 (Berlin: Töpelmann, 1953): 1–35.

Jeremias, J. *Theophanie: die Geschichte einer alttestamentlichen Gattung*. Neukirchen-Vluyn: Neukirchener Verlag, 1965.

John Chrysostom. *Homilies on Genesis*. http://www2.iath.virginia. edu/anderson/commentaries/ChrGen .html#glossGen3:2%20Gen3:3.

Kautsch, E., and A. E. Cowley, eds. *Gesenius' Hebrew Grammar*. Oxford: Clarendon, 1910.

Keener, Craig S. *Acts: An Exegetical Commentary, vol. 2: 3:1–14:28*. Grand Rapids: Baker Academic, 2013.

Keil, C. F., and F. Delitzsch. *Biblical Commentary on the Old Testament, Vol. 1, the Pentateuch*. Translated by Rev. James Martin. Edinburgh: T&T Clark, 1885.

Kidner, Derek. *Genesis: An Introduction and Commentary*. Downers Grove, IL: InterVarsity Press, 1967.

Kistemaker, Simon J. *Exposition of the Acts of the Apostles*. New Testament Commentary. Grand Rapids: Baker, 1990.

Kline, Meredith G. "Abram's *Amen*." *WTJ* 31 (1968/69): 1–11.

———. *God, Heaven, and Har Magedon: A Covenantal Tale of Cosmos and Telos*. Eugene, OR: Wipf & Stock, 2006.

———. *Kingdom Prologue: Genesis Foundations for a Covenantal Worldview*. Overland Park, KS: Two Age Press, 2000.

———. *The Structure of Biblical Authority*. Grand Rapids: Eerdmans, 1973.

König, E. *Die Genesis*. Gutersloh: Bertelsmann, 1925.

Kugel, James L. *The Bible as It Was*. Cambridge: Harvard University Press, 1997.

Kuntz, J. K. *The Self-Revelation of God*. Philadelphia: Westminster, 1967.

Lake, Kirsopp, and Henry J. Cadbury. *The Acts of the Apostles*. Part I, Vol. IV of *The Beginnings of Christianity*. Edited by F. J. Foakes Jackson and Kirsopp Lake, eds. London: Macmillan and Co., 1933.

Lewis, C. S. *Perelandra*. New York: MacMillan, 1944.

Luther, Martin. *A Critical and Devotional Commentary on Genesis*. Translated by John Nicholas Lenker. Minneapolis: Lutherans in All Lands Co., 1904.

Marshall, I. Howard. *The Acts of the Apostles: An Introduction and Commentary*. Leicester: Inter-Varsity Press, 1980.

Murphy, James G. *A Critical and Exegetical Commentary on the Book of Genesis, with a New Translation*. Boston: Estes and Lauriat, 1873.

Neusner, Jacob. *Genesis Rabbah: The Judaic Commentary to the Book of Genesis: A New American Translation*. Vol. 1. Atlanta: Scholars Press, 1985.

Niehaus, Jeffrey J. *The Common Grace Covenants*. Vol. 1 of *Biblical Theology*. Bellingham, WA: Lexham Press, 2014.

———. *God at Sinai*. Grand Rapids: Zondervan, 1995.

———. "God's Covenant with Abraham," *JETS* 56.2 (2013): 249–71.

———. *The Special Grace Covenants (New Testament)*. Vol. 3 of *Biblical Theology*. Bellingham, WA: Lexham Press, 2019.

———. *The Special Grace Covenants (Old Testament)*. Vol. 2 of *Biblical Theology*. Bellingham, WA: Lexham Press, 2018.

———. "The Warrior and His God: The Covenant Foundation of History and Historiography." Pages 299–312 in *Faith, Tradition, and History: Old Testament Historiography in Its Near Eastern Context*. Edited by A. R. Millard and James K. Hoffmeier. Winona Lake, IN: Eisenbrauns, 1994.

———. "In the Wind of the Storm: Another Look at Genesis III 8," *VT* 44.2 (1994): 263–67.

Peterson, David G. *The Acts of the Apostles*. Grand Rapids: Eerdmans, 2009.

Philo. *Questions and Answers on Genesis*. Translated by Ralph Marcus. Loeb Classical Library 380. Cambridge: Harvard University Press, 1953.

Polzin, Robert. *David and the Deuteronomist: A Literary Study of the Deuteronomistic History, Part 3*. Bloomington: Indiana University Press, 1993.

———. *Moses and the Deuteronomist: A Literary Study of the Deuteronomistic History, Part 1*. Bloomington: Indiana University Press, 1993.

———. *Samuel and the Deuteronomist: A Literary Study of the Deuteronomistic History, Part 2*. Bloomington: Indiana University Press, 1993.

Rad, Gerhard von. *Genesis: A Commentary*. 2nd ed. London: SCM, 1972.

———. *Genesis: A Commentary*. Philadelphia: Westminster John Knox Press, 1973.

Ross, Allen P. *Creation and Blessing: A Guide to the Study and Exposition of the Book of Genesis*. Grand Rapids: Baker Academic, 1988.

Ryle, Herbert E. *The Book of Genesis, The Cambridge Bible for Schools and Colleges*. Edited by A. F. Kirkpatrick. Cambridge: University Press, 1914.

Schnabel, Eckhard. *Acts*. Zondervan Exegetical Commentary on the New Testament. Grand Rapids: Zondervan, 2012.

Skinner, John. *A Critical and Exegetical Commentary on Genesis*. 2nd ed. Edinburgh: T&T Clark, 1994.

Smith, R. Payne. *Genesis*. London: Cassel & Co., Ltd., 1885.

Speiser, E. A. *Genesis*. Garden City, NY: Doubleday, 1964.

Stendahl, K. *Paul among Jews and Gentiles and Other Essays*. London: SCM Press, 1977.

Townsend, P. Wayne. "Eve's Answer to the Serpent: An Alternative Paradigm for Sin and Some Implications in Theology." *CTJ* 33 (1998): 399–420.

Van Seters, J. *Abraham in History and Tradition*. New Haven: Yale University Press, 1975.

Vos, Geerhardus. *Biblical Theology*. Grand Rapids: Eerdmans, 1975.

Waltke, Bruce K., and Cathi J. Fredricks. *Genesis: A Commentary*. Grand Rapids: Zondervan, 2001.

Walton, John H. *The IVP Bible Background Commentary: Genesis–Deuteronomy*. Downers Grove, IL: InterVarsity Press, 1997.

Wenham, Gordon. *Genesis 1–15*. WBC 1. Waco, TX: Word, 1987.

———. *Genesis 16–50*. WBC 2. Waco, TX: Word, 1994.

Westermann, Claus. *Genesis 1–11*. Biblischer Kommentar, Altes Testament, 1 i. Neukirchen-Vluyn: Neukirchener Verlag, 1976.

———. *Genesis 1–11: A Continental Commentary*. Translated by John J. Scullion, SJ. Minneapolis: Fortress, 1984.

————. *Genesis 12–36*. Biblischer Kommentar, Altes Testament, I ii.
        Neukirchen-Vluyn: Neukirchener Verlag, 1981.

————. *Genesis 12–36: A Commentary*. Translated by John. J.
        Scullion, SJ. Minneapolis: Augsburg Publishing House,
        1985.

de Wette, W. M. L. *Dissertatio Critica qua Deuteronomium diversum
        a prioribus Pentateuchi libris, alius cuiusdam recentioris
        autoris opus esse demonstratur*. Jena, 1805.

Whitelaw, Thomas. *Genesis*. In *The Pulpit Commentary, Vol. 1*.
        Grand Rapids: Eerdmans, 1950.

Witherington, Ben, III. *The Acts of the Apostles: A Socio-Rhetorical
        Commentary*. Grand Rapids: Eerdmans, 1998.

Zlotowitz, Meir. *Bereishis/Genesis: A New Translation with a
        Commentary from Talmudic, Midrashic and Rabbinic Sources*.
        Brooklyn: Mesorah Publications, 1977.